TWAYNE'S WORLD AUTHORS SERIES

A Survey of the World's Literature

Sylvia E. Bowman, Indiana University

GENERAL EDITOR

POLAND

Adam Gillon, State University of New York College
at New Paltz
Ludwik Krzyzanowski, New York University

EDITORS

Jan Parandowski

(TWAS 112)

TWAYNE'S WORLD AUTHORS SERIES (TWAS)

The purpose of TWAS is to survey the major writers —novelists, dramatists, historians, poets, philosophers, and critics—of the nations of the world. Among the national literatures covered are those of Australia, Canada, China, Eastern Europe, France, Germany, Greece, Italy, Japan, Latin America, New Zealand, Poland, Russia, Scandinavia, Spain, and the African nations, as well as Hebrew, Yiddish, and Latin Classical literature. This survey is complemented by Twayne's United States Authors Series and English Authors Series.

The intent of each volume in these series is to present a critical-analytical study of the works of the writer; to include biographical and historical material that may be necessary for understanding, appreciation, and critical appraisal of the writer; and to present all material in clear, concise English—but not to vitiate the scholarly content of the work by doing so.

Jan Parandowski

By GEORGE HARJAN

York University

Twayne Publishers, Inc. :: New York

To Dr. Philip H. Arnot
with great respect and deep gratitude

Let me not to the marriage of true minds
Admit impediments. Love is not Love
Which alters when it alteration finds,
Or bends with the remover to remove:
O no; it is an ever-fixed mark,
That looks on tempests, and is never shaken;
It is the star to every wandering bark,
Whose worth's unknown, although his height be taken.
Love's not Time's fool, though rosy lips and cheeks
Within his bending sickle's compass come;
Love alters not with his brief hours and weeks,
But bears it out even to the edge of doom.
If this be error, and upon me prov'd,
I never writ, nor no man ever lov'd.

Shakespeare, Sonnet CXVI

Preface

It was a cold and dreary autumn evening in Oklahoma when, before going home, I dropped in at the office of the international quarterly *Books Abroad*. The editor greeted me and said that he had a book for me to review. It was in Polish—a collection of works by Jan Parandowski. The name did not mean much to me; yet as I opened the book I was struck by its extraordinary, diversified contents. First, there was a novel about a young boy from Eastern Europe, which betrayed an affinity to traditional psychological novels of the later nineteenth century. Next came a larger work which at first glance promised to be as decadent and avant-garde as any book published either at the *fin-de-siècle* or at the beginning of the twentieth century. It was about Oscar Wilde, a study which could not be further away, both psychologically and geographically, from the first one. My surprise grew as I saw that the following works dealt with antiquity: Ancient Rome and Classical Greece.

Perhaps the cold Oklahoma evening enhanced this first impression. Or was it perhaps the certain naïveté in the works—frivolous, like a child's dream world, yet earnest, brilliant and erudite.

This first acquaintance led me to make some inquiries about Parandowski. A second encounter took place when I sent him a letter. My premonition was correct: soon I had a kind and thoughtful reply. The correspondence grew, even during my absences from Oklahoma and his from Poland. No matter where we were we always sent at least a postcard to each other. Thus my knowledge of the writer increased considerably. I read him avidly, published several reviews of his books and was engaged in writing an article on him. When we finally met, it was in part the result of a strange experience.

During the Summer of 1960, I was in Vienna. My visit was nearing its end, and my plans for returning to the United States were made. But one warm evening, I found myself in Grinzing, a town near Vienna, sitting in the pleasant garden of an old inn, savoring the local wine. As the twilight settled over the ancient village a strange feeling came over me as though I were in a setting that was somehow familiar. Then I realized that Grinzing had evoked in me the spirit and atmosphere of the old Austro-Hungarian Empire in which Parandowski spent the childhood which he has described in so many fine pages. As a result of this experience, I changed my travel plans, went the next day to the Polish Embassy in Vienna and, after a telephone conversation with Parandowski, obtained a visa for Poland.

Thus we met. I looked with great curiosity at this man whom I had known for three years through his books. My stay was brief and, as in any such encounter, I did not learn much more about the author whom I thought I knew quite intimately.

I was aware of his importance in Polish and world literature. Parandowski is a popular writer in Poland, and has been translated into many languages. In September 1962 he celebrated the fiftieth anniversary of his first publication. He is also President of the Polish PEN Club, a position he has held for over thirty years. He can be called a contemporary Polish humanist. Though his contribution to Polish literature is considerable, it was not entirely through literature that Parandowski exerted his influence. He was and is a propagandist of the values of antiquity. Several generations of high-school children in Poland have been brought up on his *Mythology*. Many articles and reviews were written about him before and after the war; in 1957 the greatness of his literary production was in hot debate. Yet not a single biography of the author exists.

Thus my conviction grew that he deserved a study more extensive than any series of articles. The present book is an attempt to place Parandowski's life and creative output against the background of the social and literary trends of Polish letters.

In 1962 the University of Toronto made a fourth encounter possible for me. I spent two months in Warsaw, and was fortunate enough to be able to talk to the author almost every day. I also interviewed his colleagues, among them the Chairman of

Preface

the Union of Polish Writers, Jaroslaw Iwaszkiewicz; Jerzy Andrzejewski, whose novel *Ashes and Diamonds* made him well-known in North America; the playright Ludwik H. Morstin, Jan Izydor Sztaudinger, Jerzy Putrament, Wojciech Natanson and many others. I spoke with the president of the Austrian PEN Club, Franz Theodor Csokor, who knows Parandowski intimately. I also saw members of Parandowski's family, particularly his charming and indefatigable wife, Irena. Above all other acknowledgements, my gratitude is primarily directed to the author himself who was forced at times to relive his life and who, although a rather shy and reticent person, granted me the essential assistance in writing about his life and work.

Acknowledgments

The origins of this book may be ascribed to the encouragement I received at the Universities of California and Toronto; the completion owes much to York University. I gratefully express my acknowledgement for assistance given by Professor Herbert E. Bowman (University of Toronto), Professor Zbigniew Folejewski (University of British Columbia) and particularly the late Professor Waclaw Lednicki (University of California) who initiated and guided me in Slavic studies. The Humanities and Social Studies grant of the University of Toronto, provided welcome assistance for travel expenses. York University, through the Research Grants Committee and the Faculty of Arts and Science provided research grants for work in progress. The Union of Polish Writers, and the International PEN Center, made my travels in Europe pleasurable and profitable. The great assistance I have received from the Parandowski family and from several Polish writers I acknowledge in the Preface. I express my thanks to Professors Harry Girling and Lester J. Pronger, and to Mrs. Ellen Devine for assistance in correcting copy, and to Mrs. Monique Gyalokay and Miss Paule Ruffieux, for some strenuous typing.

Contents

Chronology

1895   In Lwow, on May 11, Jan Parandowski was born to Jan and Julia Parandowski.

1905-   Parandowski pursued his secondary school education in
1912   Lwow, spent his summers with his family in Italy, and began to write poetry.

1912-   Parandowski's sketches on Krasinski and Rousseau pub-
1913   lished; graduated from school.

1914   Travelled alone to Italy, and began studies at Lwow University.

1915   In July, Parandowski was forced to leave Lwow by the retreating Russians who had occupied the city at the beginning of World War I. He spent the war years at Saratov on the Volga.

1918-   Parandowski returned to Lwow and to the University;
1923   worked in the *Gazeta Lwowska;* published *Antinous in the Velvet Beret* and *The Sorcerers of Rome.*

1923   Publication of *Mythology* and *Eros on Olympus.* Parandowski became an editor for *Altenberg.*

1924   Parandowski met Irena Helzel.

1925   First trip to Greece resulting in *Aspasia,* a portrait of Pericles's wife. Translation of *Daphnis and Chloe.* Marriage to Irena.

1926   Trip to Sicily and Capri.

1927   Publication of *Two Springs.*

1930   Publication of *King of Life.* Parandowski moved to Warsaw with his wife, daughter and son and, for a time, edited *Pamietnik Warszawski.*

1932   Another trip to Greece resulting in the publication of *The Olympic Discus.*

1933   In December, Parandowski was elected president of the Polish PEN Club. In this capacity, he travelled to the prewar International Congresses in Edinburgh (1934), Buenos-Aires (1936), and Paris (1937).

1935   Publication of *The Adventures of Odysseus* and of Parandowski's only true novel, *Heaven in Flames*.

1936- At the Olympic Games in Berlin, Parandowski was
1937   awarded a bronze medal for his *Olympic Discus*.

1939   *Three Signs of the Zodiac* and *Meetings and Encounters* were published. The first English edition of *The Olympic Discus* appeared just as the war broke out. The Parandowskis, seeking safety and work for the war years, moved first to Lublin and then to Strzyzewice, and finally back to Warsaw.

1942- The family found refuge in the village of Planta.
1944

1944   In July, the front line moved to Planta. The Parandowskis fled from the middle of the battle, first to Tarnobrzeg where their second son Piotr was born, then to an estate near Lublin. Parandowski became head of the new department of comparative literature at Lublin Catholic University, finally returning to Warsaw to teach.

1945- New editions of *Three Signs of the Zodiac, Two Springs,*
1948   *Heaven in Flames* and *Olympic Discus* appeared.

1946   Parandowski attended the first postwar PEN Club congress in Sweden.

1949   Publication of *Mediterranean Hour*. Parandowski attended the PEN Club congress in Venice.

1950   Parandowski resigned his professorship at Lublin.

1951   Publication of *Alchemy of the Word*.

1953   Publication of *Sundial*, a series of sketches from Parandowski's youth.

1954   Publication of *Petrarch*.

1955   Publication of *The Art of Translating* to which Parandowski contributed, and of the first anthology of Parandowski's works, *Selected Writings*.

1958   Publication of *My Literary Travels* and *The Third Spring*.

1959   Parandowski was awarded Order of *Polonia Restituta*.

1960   Publication of *Juvenilia*.

1961   Publication of *Return to Life*.

Chronology

1962   Publication of *September Night.*
1963   The Polish Government bestowed upon Parandowski the Banner of Labor Order.
1966   Recipient of Alfred Jurzykowski Foundation Millennium Award in New York.

CHAPTER 1

The Beginnings

IN 1895 the city of Lwow was the bustling center of the north-
eastern part of the Austro-Hungarian Empire. The Austrians
called it Lemberg. Most of its population of 130,000 was Polish,
but its sizeable Jewish and Ukrainian communities and the fact
that it was the seat of the Greek-Catholic Metropolitan gave it
a cosmopolitan atmosphere.

Here on May 11, 1895, Jan Parandowski was born. The city had
much to offer the small boy. Its colorful past, mirrored in its
historical monuments—the Roman Catholic cathedral, an Ar-
menian cathedral in Byzantine style, the Greek-Catholic cathedral
of Saint George, the old city hall, and the ruins of an ancient
castle dominating the city from the highest of its hills—surely
caught the imagination of a sensitive child.

The city's cultural life also contributed to the young man's
experience. It had a good theater founded in 1843 by Count
Skarbek, in which Polish dramas and Italo-Polish operas were
presented. There was the University, founded in the seventeenth
century, which was Germanized by the Austrians after the first
partition of Poland, but re-Polanized in the 1870's when Polish
became the language of instruction. Lwow also had several
secondary schools, one of which Parandowski was to attend.
One of the most important institutions was the famous National
Ossolinski Institute, "Ossolineum," founded in 1818, with a magnificent library, archives, museum, and a renowned publishing
house of Polish scholarly works. This institute was to make an
important contribution to Parandowski's development.

Parandowski's father was a civil servant, a class that pre-
dominated in the city although commerce and industry were
well-developed. Parandowski is reticent about discussing his

father; he does not remember him, for he was only two when his father died.

Two people are important in Parandowski's childhood: his mother, Julia, and his paternal grandmother, née Grodzicka. Parandowski used the name later in his *Heaven in Flames*. In his *Sundial* Parandowski constantly alludes to his grandmother— a great patriot, with a serene countenance, kind and strict at the same time. Born in 1810, she died at the venerable age of 98. Poland went through a turbulent period in the life span of Parandowski's grandmother. Although she was reluctant to talk about herself, Parandowski remembers from her talk that she must have helped the insurgents in the uprising of 1830-31 and certainly the insurgents of 1863. Parandowski says that the family often had mysterious callers, people whom she helped during the uprising. She also must have known some of the literary figures; in one of her conversations she mentioned that she knew Aleksander Fredro (1793-1876), the popular playwright, quite well.[1]

It would be safe to assume that Parandowski's childhood was a happy one. In due time he enrolled in one of the secondary schools, which he remembers with great affection. Number 4, later to be called "Jan Dlugosz Gymnasium" in honor of the great fifteenth century Polish historian, was a strict classical institution. The future author was a bright but somewhat lazy and boisterous student. Having failed his Greek examination in grade six, he had to repeat it in the fall—from this time arose his interest in Homer and a general interest in the classical languages. The instruction was kept on a very high level, and he became more and more engrossed in classical philology—an interest enhanced no doubt by his summer trips to Italy, to the small island of Grado and to Venice. Otherwise, the life and the formative years which the author was to describe so brilliantly in his *Sundial* went by uneventfully. Nothing perturbed the family. No one suspected the forthcoming events.

Near the end of his high-school days Parandowski began to write. As he remembers in his *Moje poczatki literackie* (My Literary Beginnings), he paid his tribute to poetry, trying his hand at exotic material. Soon, however, he turned to prose. The year of 1912 had two memorable dates—the anniversaries of Zygmunt Krasinski (1812-1859), one of the great Polish

Romanticists, who together with Adam Mickiewicz (1798-1855) and Juliusz Slowacki (1809-1849) formed the "Great Polish Literary Trinity," and that of Jean-Jacques Rousseau. Parandowski wrote for both, but it was his study of Rousseau that made him known in the world of letters. His literary and philosophical sketch appeared in book form a few weeks before Parandowski's graduation. What a wonderful time it must have been for the young boy. As the author remarks, there is nothing that can be compared to the first proofreading of one's first book. According to Parandowski's wish, all the copies of the book were sent to the bookseller Altenberg—a man who later published Parandowski and whose book-store the young man knew well. The price for each copy was set at one crown; what a pleasant surprise it was when the young author was rewarded with 300 crowns. Previously, editors had usually paid him by giving him free theatre tickets or a first-class railroad ticket. Now, "When I walked on Akademicka Street, it seemed to be strewn with diamonds."² Later, when Parandowski was working as a literary editor for the same company, he realized how lucky he was to have been so handsomely rewarded.

In his mature years, Parandowski calls his study of Rousseau an immature work belonging to his juvenilia. He claims this was not really his literary beginning; nevertheless it was eagerly discussed at the time. One curious review praised the study as a work by a man well-known as a journalist.

It is symptomatic of Parandowski's career that his first literary essay deals with a writer and a philosopher—a topic which will recur often in his later creative activity. The sketch on Rousseau betrays other traits which are characteristic of the later Parandowski. It is concise, and written in a clear, simple, yet elegant style. The work is not monumental but shows a sobriety amazing for a boy of seventeen.

In the summer of 1914 Parandowski went to Rome, alone for the first time. This trip, a graduation present from his mother, was his second encounter with the Eternal City, and it developed into a lasting and permanent friendship. The voyage must have been exciting for a carefree youth. He recalls that it was his fancy to stay at a hotel of the same name in every city. The name young Parandowski chose was "Metropole." In Vienna, his first stop, he found the Metropole to be an extremely fashionable hotel. He was invited to visit some of the other guests—most of them princes or counts—and the management had special visiting cards printed for him. In Bologna the Metropole was not as elegant, but in Rome it was excellent. In Milan he was asked whether he would like to go to a casino. He had never gambled; furthermore he had no white tie. Everything was provided for him in the shortest possible time. He played, and it seemed that fortune accompanied him everywhere—he won. The Metropole also provided him with a magnificent carriage. He had decided at the beginning of his trip not to carry any baggage; when he went away, he left his laundry and all the clothes he had acquired at the hotel. Small wonder that in spite of a generous allowance from his mother, he had to wire for more money as soon as he reached Rome.

Parandowski always considered these travel experiences as a genuine *fin-de-siècle* escapade, one of the pleasures of youth. But is was also profitable, for in spite of his frivolous adventures he was receptive to everything around him. Florence made an indelible impression on him. Later, in calmer years, all this found its expression in his work on the Italian Renaissance. Such escapades are frowned on nowadays, but Europe has gone through two horrible wars since that time. We are perhaps wiser through suffering, but the light-minded giddiness and charm of those years is gone.

In the fall of the same year Parandowski enrolled at the University of Lwow and began to study classical philology, philosophy, archaeology and Oriental studies, out of which grew his considerable love and knowledge of classical Hebrew. Much later, in his *Reminiscences and Profiles*, he wrote that he took his studies very seriously. In fact the registration official smiled at the extensive list of courses which Parandowski planned to attend. The young student soon saw himself embracing an academic career.

Parandowski's student life was uneventful. He even succeeded in remaining aloof from the political ferment that was the prelude to the approaching cataclysm. His unperturbed life was soon shattered, however, when World War I began. The beginning of the war caught him at Grado reading Plato (a symbolic coincidence), but he quickly returned to Lwow, shortly to be occupied by Russian troops. In July 1915, suffering reverses on other fronts, the Russians had to move out of the city—a retreat which was to change Parandowski's life. Since he was of draft age and the Russians wished to keep him out of the Austrian army, he was ordered to leave with them.

Thus began his Russian adventure—an odyssey which was to last almost to the end of the war. Parandowski was first taken to Volhynia, later to Voronezh, and finally to Saratov on the Volga River. He was treated fairly well, learned to speak Russian and earned a little money to supplement what his mother sent him, through the International Red Cross. He also received considerable aid and assistance from so-called Polish committees which were supported by a great Polish patriot in Russia, Aleksander Lednicki. Scattered from Moscow to Kiev and from Armavir to Saratov and on to Tomsk and Chita, they rendered invaluable assistance to Poles stranded in Russia. Aside from outright financial and medical assistance, they instituted grade and high schools, as well as courses of higher education.[3] Parandowski taught at one of the numerous schools. We know that he did not completely abandon his literary activity. Stimulated by the reading of Sienkiewicz's *Quo Vadis?* Parandowski wrote *Chelidon*, a sketch on a topic from antiquity. This short work, written in 1916, was published in 1919.

At the outbreak of the Russian Revolution and the beginning of the Civil War, we find Parandowski moving slowly towards Lwow. Like many Poles around him, Parandowski was aided by the Polish Repatriation Commission also organized by the indefatigable Aleksander Lednicki.[4] He arrived just in time to watch his city go through a new crisis.

Although Lwow at that time was inhabited predominantly by Poles, historically, it belonged to so-called Red Rus' and had been founded by Galician princes. Many of its inhabitants thought of themselves as Ukrainians and regarded Lwow as a Ukrainian city. While the Poles were rejoicing at their coming independence, the Ukrainians planned a coup. They struck on November 1, 1918. The Polish population rallied to fight these Ukrainian forces and expelled the Ukrainian nationalists from the city.[5] Parandowski was in the city when the fighting broke out, but he never joined the battle. Exhausted after an extensive and arduous journey, Parandowski fell victim to influenza—an illness which had reached epidemic proportions. He remembers those days as in a haze. There was a din of cannon, crackling of rifles and rattling of machine guns, but most of the time, he says, he was in a state of delirium.

In spite of the privations, life went on. Parandowski recovered and in 1919 was able to begin anew his university studies. The first lectures were held under artillery bombardment.

I *Literary Beginnings*

The twentieth anniversary of the death of Oscar Wilde was commemorated by the Union of Polish Writers on November 30, 1920 and for this occasion Parandowski was invited to present a lecture. This was followed by a reading of *The Ballad of Reading Gaol*, by the talented actor Janusz Kozlowski. The evening dedicated to Wilde was so successful that it had to be repeated and Parandowski was requested to submit his lecture for publication.

That is how a small volume entitled *Antinous w aksamitnym berecie* (Antinous in the Velvet Beret) was produced. This early sketch is a poetical outline of the life and work of Oscar Wilde whose aestheticism and brilliance of style greatly appealed to the young Parandowski. He encountered some difficulties in obtaining the necessary research material and, as he later admitted, committed several errors of fact. Nevertheless the sketch was a worthy tribute to a tormented poet who was much in vogue at that time in Poland. Parandowski drew a parallel between classic and modern cultures, showing Wilde as a new manifestation of the spirit of Dionysus.[6]

Another work published somewhat later, in 1922, was likewise written for an occasion. Again a lecture was presented at the Union of Writers and further developed, this time into *Rzym czarodziejski* (The Sorcerers of Rome). Like *Eros na Olimpie* (Eros on Olympus) the *Rzym* is a by-product of the work he was doing on his *Mitologia*. In this curious sketch Parandowski relates, as an amusing story, the history of black magic from ancient Rome well into the Middle Ages.

An interesting episode took place during the reading of the lecture. Parandowski's audience was becoming somewhat restless until one man got up and told the people not to worry. "I have seen similar performances before," he said, "first he reads

and after this he will perform." Thus the audience was dis-
appointed when at the end of the lecture Parandowski did not
perform as a magician himself.

In 1923-24 Parandowski was one of the editors of *Gazeta
Lwowska,* a newspaper to which he also often contributed
essays and articles. About this time he finished his formal
education at the University of Lwow. Though still retaining a
keen interest in antiquity, he was beginning to find little profit
in the lectures of some of his professors and felt he had out-
grown them. Furthermore, he wished to devote more of his
time to writing, being now quite convinced that he would be
a professional writer, rather than an academic. He likewise
needed more time to cultivate new interests arising from his
study of antiquity, namely numismatics and sphragistics.

Another result of this study was the publication, in 1923, of
his *Mythology,* dealing with the beliefs and traditions of ancient
Greeks and Romans. Parandowski had always felt that he would
one day write this book; even as a schoolboy he had bought
the magnificent Roscher encyclopedia of classical Greece and
Rome. His *Mythology,* a very complete treatment of the subject,
was destined for young readers. Its success was instantaneous;
the first edition was sold out at once—but purchased by adults
rather than young people. One well-known scholar, Kazimierz
Czachowski, attributed its success to Parandowski's skill in
fashioning a "textbook" into a magnificent, colorful story.[7]

Parandowski's increasing productivity at this time resulted
in the appearance of yet another book in 1923, *Eros on Olympus,*
a collection of eleven short stories dealing with amorous escapades of the immortals. Without being salacious, the book is
frivolously erotic and quite amusing. As Parandowski remembers,
he was tired of castrating his gods; he felt that he had wasted
too much good literary material. His august characters emerge
as lovable beings with human frailties due to the author's sym-
pathetic attitude towards them as well as his graceful style and
subtle all-pervading humor. A certain affinity with *The Dialogues
of the Gods* and *The Dialogues of the Sea-Gods* as well as with
The Council of the Gods of Lucian, in the form as well as in
the treatment of the subject matter, can be detected in this
charming collection. The dialogue form is to play an important
role in Parandowski's later literary activity. The author is

particularly indebted to Ovid's *Metamorphoses,* among other sources.[8]

Altenberg, Parandowski's first publisher, invited him to join his staff, and Parandowski became a literary editor. Several projects can be attributed to his vigorous editorship. The first was to be a series by the name of *Propyleje,* a library dedicated to great men in culture. This project, however, according to the words of Parandowski, remained purely in conversation and in his head. Instead appeared a series, *Wielcy pisarze* (Great Writers), inaugurated by a magnificent volume on *Mikolaj Rej* (1505-1569), "the father" of modern Polish literature, by Alexander Brückner, which was followed by a more modest one on Mickiewicz by Marian Szyjkowski.

Parandowski by now was well established as a journalist and a writer and had translated *Daphnis and Chloe;* shortly after, he wrote another short work, *Aspazja* (Aspasia 1925). Again it was conceived as one of a series of biographies, this time of famous women, to be published by Altenberg. Tadeusz Boy-Zelenski (1874-1941) had begun the series with a work about Madame Hanska, Balzac's wife. *Aspasia* is a literary miniature. In some twenty-five pages, Parandowski wrote a poetical biography of Pericles' wife. It is indeed amazing how much material the writer was able to incorporate into this literary gem in which he admirably recreates the atmosphere and the setting of Athens during the Golden Age of Pericles. He showed the struggle of this brilliant woman to assert herself in a rigid society and all the influence of her strong, noble and perhaps tragic character. What is more striking, Parandowski was able to create her physical portrait. It is difficult to judge how true to life this portrait is—we have only one portrait in marble at the Vatican museum, yet the writer showed an amazing perspicacity, incisiveness and subtle poetical tact. But then perhaps it was not a coincidence that Parandowski was susceptible to feminine beauty at that time. In 1924 Parandowski met his future wife, Irena.

One of Parandowski's close friends and collaborators, Ludwik H. Morstin, once commented that it would be easy to write about the personal life of Parandowski. The man who devoted so much time and effort to depict love affairs of the Immortals on Olympus as well as of ordinary mortals in everyday life had an uneventful life in this respect. True, there were some "visits and encounters," but they were of a secondary nature and did not, with the exception of one, go beyond a "casual fruition." Parandowski's wife was his only true love, and their relationship was of exceptional stability. By no means a question of Tolstoyan "family happiness," it and the influence of Irena rather reminds one of the role of Snitkina, the wife of Dostoyevsky. Parandowski could not have made a better choice. Madame Parandowska claims that intuitively she felt what the role of a writer's wife should be. The life was exacting, for a writer is by necessity a selfish man. This can be said in retrospect. It seems that the first sentiment of that young girl was genuine, and probably first love. This first love turned into a fascinating friendship and collaboration, and a selfless devotion. It was not easy, this amazing foresight, this self-immersion and blending with another individual. There were sacrifices. Madame Parandowska became a wife, a friend, and, as often happens, a secretary.

Irena Helzel, the future Mrs. Parandowska, was born in Lwow. Her father, who had a small art gallery, had been a singer and a disciple of a famous Vienna court musician, Hermann Wienckelmann. After he lost his voice, he was forced to abandon his career, but he saw that his daughter acquired a solid musical education. Her mother, Franziska, née Szeps, was also educated in Vienna. Irena was quite adroit at the piano, but all this came to an end when she met Parandowski. When Parandowski went to Paris in 1924 and, in the spring of 1925, to Greece, he wrote her volumes of love letters. In the fall of 1925 they were married in the Church of St. Nicholas.

II *The Contemporaries*

We have touched upon the beginnings of Parandowski's literary activity and the main traits are apparent. They show the parallel development of an interest in antiquity, a desire to popularize mythology, and an interest in biography. Yet Parandowski never creates an ordinary biography; it is more like poetical musing or philosophical reflection. This is what his sketch on Rousseau and his study of Oscar Wilde came to be.

Many years later Parandowski claimed that he stood aloof from the general development of Polish literature of the 1920's, at the same time admitting that his work was a natural outcome of Polish literary tradition. He was deeply involved with all contemporary Polish writers through his activities with the Polish PEN Club. What then was the literary tradition in Poland after the country regained national and cultural independence? According to a well-known scholar, Wilhelm Feldman, contemporary to the proclamation of independence, the political rebirth of Poland failed to bring about a harmonious flowering of Polish letters. Of course, Poland was beset by many economic and political problems; it had gone through a severe war, and a fratricidal civil war was brewing. It would, however, be wrong to assume that literature was stifled; on the contrary, many groups and factions were formed and many art and literary schools were organized. Parandowski considered himself a critical realist yet his position was peculiar because of his preoccupation with antiquity. During the 1920's, however, antiquity was a popular theme in the Polish theater with which Parandowski was connected as a critic. The works of Tadeusz Zielinski, a great Polish classical scholar and writer, certainly inspired Parandowski, as probably also did the poetry of Leopold Staff. Like Parandowski, Staff was interested in antiquity and in sculpture; like him, Staff thought in terms of the plasticity of his images.

Polish prose was less subjected to foreign influences than poetry.[9] According to Parandowski himself, two Polish writers influenced him at that time. He obtained his historicism and style from Henryk Sienkiewicz, and an interest in urban life from Boleslaw Prus (1847-1912), called "The Polish Dickens." Stefan Zeromski (1864-1925), however, was too baroque for Parandowski.

CHAPTER 2

Two Springs *and* King of Life

Whan that Aprill with his shoures soote
The droghte of March hath perced to the roote,
And bathed every veyne in swich licour
Of which vertu engendred is the flour;
Whan Zephirus eek with his sweete breeth
Inspired hath in every holt and heeth
The tendre croppes, and the yonge sonne
Hath in the Ram his halve cours yronne,
And smale foweles maken melodye,
That slepen al the nyght with open ye
(So priketh hem nature in hir corages);
Thanne longen folk to goon on pilgrimages.

—Chaucer

I Two Springs

IN 1926-27 Parandowski wrote a work which was later to be
celebrated as a masterpiece and which firmly established
his position and reputation in contemporary Polish literature.
Dwie wiosny (Two Springs) is a cumulative result of some
previous energetic literary activity and of two trips, one in 1925
to Greece, another in 1926 to Sicily and to the island of Capri.
As the author states in the preface to his 1952 edition, he did
not think about writing the book at the time of his travels. He
did not take notes, nor did he keep a journal of any kind.
After he decided that he must compose the book, all of his
impressions and images began to assemble in his mind.

The word "compose" is most fitting, for *Two Springs* has an
almost symphonic quality about it. It was just as well, Parandowski states, that he did not write the book during his travels.

Everything that was merely incidental was forgotten; only the joyous, happy and memorable events remained. The process of writing and of contemplation led Parandowski back into his childhood and to the first awakening of his interest in antiquity. *Two Springs* is an evocative and partly retrospective work.

The book is closely related to the author's *Mythology*, but its setting is realistic. The form has existed since Ovid and Apuleius, which is not to say that Parandowski's work is imitative. It is an original creation, a curious blend of realism and romanticism interlaced with the classical elements of the author's thought and style.

Two Springs abounds in memories of antiquity, yet the book is national in its character. Nostalgically, the writer leaves Poland, then returns to it and to "the great Polish spring." Reading *Two Springs*, one cannot help remembering Mickiewicz's *Crimean Sonnets*, and one is almost tempted to believe that Parandowski was thinking about them as he wrote. Both cycles are essentially the stories of peregrination in foreign and exotic lands; both cycles evoke memories of youth and of Poland. To Parandowski, the classicist, antiquity becomes just as important as some distant and far-off place becomes for Mickiewicz, the romanticist. For both poets the voyage is a personal experience. The same sense of movement and motion is characteristic of both cycles.

Parandowski was able to create a total image of Greece; the reader has an almost physical perception not only of the country-side but of the ancient world. Parandowski achieves this, after a short introduction, as soon as he begins to describe his voyage. He arrives in Greece, and the landscape slowly unfolds itself before the reader's eyes. First, he gives a description of a rock on the horizon, which becomes Athens. The focal point is the rock, which is soon transformed into the Acropolis; then the focus becomes the Parthenon. His chapter, "The Heavenly Capital," is perhaps the best example of how Parandowski develops an image from the general to the particular and back again.

After introducing the Parthenon, the author gives a detailed description of the columns, caryatids and the whole building. But the Parthenon he shows us is not the one he actually saw in the 1920's; it is the Parthenon we would have seen 2,000 years ago. If the details are missing in a contemporary view,

the author fills them in from his knowledge of architecture and
from his rich, fertile imagination. Then the picture of the
Parthenon grows beyond the scope of the edifice: a description
of a small museum next to the Parthenon leads to a discussion of
the Greek genius in general. Parandowski achieves great plasticity in his delineation and presentation of the sculptures of
Praxiteles and Phidias.

Here too, the pattern of the writer's narrative is strict, from
the general to the detail and from the physical to the spiritual.
After describing the material culture of Ancient Greece, Parandowski moves on to the poetry of Sophocles. This time he moves
from the detail and again creates an imposing picture of the
Parthenon, interspersed with personal digressions. Once the
image of the Parthenon is firmly established in one's mind, the
author concludes his essay by giving a bird's eye view of the
city, *urbs beata,* a symbol of contemporary creativity. The conclusion of this chapter is an all-embracing discussion of Greek
culture: "The culture of Greece is embodied in that heavenly
capital which made it immortal." From architecture we move
to drama and the dialogues of Plato.

Having thus established the center in this panorama, the author
moves into the countryside as well as into the history of the
country. The road becomes an all-important continuing image;
the names of several chapters show this. The author walks or
begins his stories, "Having taken a cane in my hand . . ." or
"I set out for a . . ." or "The train moved . . . ." Each journey
has its destination and its end, but we also imperceptibly move
on from one trip to another. The writer gives us a very detailed
account of Greek landscape and of the people in particular.
Thus, as in the case of "The Heavenly Capital," the author
moves from the concrete to the historical and back to concrete
reality. A chapter entitled "The Mystic Road" is a good
example. First comes the walk amidst the old streets, but almost
at once there is a reference to ancient times, then on with
the walk and back again to antiquity. This process gives the
writer the time and means to develop his thoughts on the
earthiest of all the goddesses, Demeter, and the occasion to
conclude the chapter by drawing parallels, pointing out the
similarity of Christian legend to the myth about the god-bearing
mother.

It is curious to note that although he depicts the countryside, Parandowski is far from being bucolic. The general tenor of the book is far removed from the spirit of an idyll. Nevertheless, being on the road, for Parandowski, is always a joyous occasion. There is in it a sense of discovery and intrigue. The whole beginning of "Kalimera," an encounter with a little girl, is almost entirely a lyrical digression, and then suddenly—almost abruptly—another digression into antiquity.

Two Springs began with a description of the everlasting and eternal sea. It is with the sea that the cycle ends. The voyage is at an end, and the author anticipates his return to Poland with its completely different climate and surroundings. It is an anticipation of the modest but great Polish spring. The conclusion is perhaps one of the richest, most lyrical and most regal examples of Polish prose. The style is all important in *Two Springs*. With few exceptions Parandowski uses short sentences which with the rising and falling sequence of events becomes almost rhythmical and at times reads like poetry. In the collection there are eleven stories; with the introduction, these total twelve items which in the manner of their organization remind one of a sonnet. The construction and conclusion of this charming book prompted some critics to call it a sonnet-like collection.

II King of Life

After the publication of *Two Springs* there was an upsurge in Parandowski's creative activity. In the years 1928-29 he wrote another book which takes the reader into a completely different society. It is a *vie romancée* of his old subject, Oscar Wilde, though some contemporary critics preferred to call it an essay because of Parandowski's established reputation as an essayist.

Krol zycia (King of Life), seemingly far removed from the Greek soil, has upon closer investigation a subtle affinity with it. Parandowski enjoys the study of great personalities, and has already written *Aspasia* and a sketch on Rousseau. After working for some time on a biography of Socrates and a novel entitled *Caligula*, both unfinished, Parandowski turned to the controversial character of Oscar Wilde.

Parandowski was aided by two circumstances: first, Wilde was a highly popular writer in Poland; second, the subject was not new to Parandowski. We remember his *Antinous in the Velvet*

Beret. King of Life is a considerably more mature work and added significantly to Parandowski's reputation. There is also a purely accidental reason why Parandowski was prompted to write about Wilde. As early as 1921, Altenberg had announced that within the year, a publication of the collected works of Oscar Wilde would appear under the editorship of Parandowski.

This was a somewhat exaggerated promise; after a few months Altenberg, as well as everybody else concerned, found that there were too many problems involved in such an undertaking, among others the question of the copyright. Parandowski then wrote to Robert Ross, the executor of Wilde's will, as well as to Vivian Holland, the poet's son. Mr. Holland answered rather cryptically that everything pertaining to the effects of Mr. Wilde should be referred to certain solicitors. Nothing came of the venture save a volume of poetry ably translated by Jan Kasprowicz (1860-1926), and the last volume of the proposed edition, a monograph by Parandowski. But these both appeared many years later and Altenberg was not to see them.

"Perhaps it was a mistake to write about such a controversial figure at that time," recalls Parandowski. He had some difficulty in obtaining the necessary material. "Nowadays it would be so much easier; no one finds any embarrassment in talking about Oscar Wilde, and all possible accounts are published." Nevertheless Parandowski did not grope entirely in darkness. Numerous accounts of the trial by friends and eyewitnesses were published on the Continent, and there was also a book of memoirs of Wilde published in the United States by Frank Harris, whose reputation was so scandalous that the book was not republished for several decades. Parandowski did some conscientious research on the Pre-Raphaelite school of painting and poetry which had influenced Wilde and was able to obtain a transcript of Oscar Wilde's trial. Numerous friends in England were able to supply Parandowski with other valuable information.

King of Life is a great improvement over *Antinous;* the latter, according to the author himself, is an immature work written in what he calls his "ornate and eloquent" style. Yet a comparison helps us to see the progress in Parandowski's creative talent. The book, essentially an *apologia* for Wilde, was perhaps best understood and appreciated as such at the time of its publication. We know more about Wilde now than at the time of Parandowski's writing. The work was undoubtedly inspired in part by the author's abiding interest in analyzing the synthesis of the old and the new; the fusing of ancient art with its reflection and outcome in modern times always fascinated Parandowski. Thus Wilde's preoccupation with ancient Greece held him spellbound. This work was called an essay but we might perhaps call it a prose-poem—a poem, not because it adheres to poetical canons, but because of its epic quality. Viewed not as a narrative but for its moral and ethical content, the work can be split into three parts: paradise lost, purgatory, and hell, all within the framework of a biography.

The story has a realistic setting, a point which should be strongly stressed. Parandowski begins his study, as all biographies should begin, with an account of Wilde's parents. The narrative is calm, with little emphasis on the scandals in the life of Wilde's father. Then follows a description of the young Wilde, his education, university studies, his friendships, his likes and dislikes. The style, even, calm, ordered and almost ponderous is in great contrast to the shrill, sensational, journalistic tone which colors the reminiscences of Frank Harris. The reader is lulled by the calm of Parandowski's account, but he has a rude awakening later on.

The author goes step by step in his description of the life of Oscar Wilde, the brilliant *causeur,* the man endowed with a great sensibility and great perception of everything beautiful. Oscar's father dies and he goes to Greece, the cradle of European civilization. From that time on his poetry again and again evokes images of ancient Greece. The poet moves to London and gradually finds a place of favor in the best social circles. Although there had been a propensity to pederasty during his childhood, Wilde the dandy now had a love affair with an actress who will later become Sybil Vane in *The Picture of Dorian Gray.* The fame of his wit spread and he made a lecture tour in the United States, adressing the students of Harvard University as well as audiences in remote towns of the West. Even his "tobacco-chewing audiences" were charmed by his brilliant wit.

Upon his return to London, Wilde the playwright, accidentally and almost under duress, created a play which made him immortal. The description of the staging of the play is one of the most poignant passages in the book. Parandowski, a theater

critic in his own right, presents an impressionistic picture. The
reader sees the stage from the point of view of the audience,
the viewer. It is not the analysis of the play but the visual effect
achieved by Parandowski which is so striking. *Lady Windermere's
Fan* is the pinnacle of Wilde's success. It not only establishes his
reputation, a fact which is to become a burden for him at the
subsequent trial, but also gives him the means for independent
livelihood.

Wilde always required more money than he possessed. Parandowski describes all the follies of the poet, beginning with his
decadence, his extreme aestheticism, a lust for life which is no
longer an elemental but a super-refined lust. Oscar Wilde is a
gourmet and a gourmand, an extravagant dandy and a collector
of meaningless though beautiful bric-à-brac. He is a bibliophile
and a collector of books on culinary science. No longer is he
satisfied with good wines; they must be excellent, rare and exotic.

But then comes a premonition of danger: the thunder clouds
are gathering, and we move into purgatory. Wilde, the poet,
King of Life, a brilliant wit and dispenser of paradoxes, meets
Alfred Douglas. Oscar's marriage is not a happy one; his wife
can by no means satisfy him intellectually. Small wonder then
that the poet and Douglas, a youth of incomparable beauty and
sensitivity, become inseparable. There is no doubt in Parandowski's mind—the author stated this on several occasions—that
Alfred Douglas, a poet, perhaps even more refined than Oscar
himself, becomes Wilde's evil genius. Douglas is Dorian Gray
come to life; the portrait appears *avant la lettre,* so to say.
This perhaps is an explanation and the key to Parandowski's
motive in choosing Wilde as the subject for his speculations.
Among other circumstantial stimuli, it is the Hellenism and the
cult of the intellect which fascinated Parandowski. The limita-
tions of one's desire are simply an impediment on the road of
progress. Aesthetics is above ethics—this is the essence of Oscar
Wilde's tragedy.

Gone now is the epic calm of Parandowski's narrative. His
style becomes abrupt and nervous, aptly conveying the hysterical
outcries of Douglas, the darling boy, the capricious *mignon* who
proves to be Wilde's undoing. It is Douglas who compels Wilde
to pick up the gauntlet and sue Lord Queensberry, a blunder
which leads the poet from the role of the accuser into the dock

of the accused. The culmination of this modern tragedy is the trial of Oscar Wilde. But his real trial begins somewhat later. We move into the circles of the inferno—Wilde against Her Majesty's court and Wilde in Her Majesty's prison, with all the inhuman treatment, degradation and exorcism.

What historical irony that one British bard is driven from the country that claims to foster both the classical tradition and freedom, to die for the freedom of Greece, and another admirer of Greece is ostracized from society, his name not to be mentioned. The later drinks the hemlock and walks the road to Golgotha. It is not the trial by Her Majesty's court but the trial by the mob, the self-satisfied mediocrities who scream "crucify him," which Parandowski judges and condemns. The jail scenes, the spiritual transformation and well-being of Oscar Wilde are reminiscent of Dostoyevsky's hero from the *Notes of the House of the Dead.*

The trials of the poet are not over even with the termination of incarceration. He is released and there is a ray of hope. Wilde is not broken, he creates; his *De Profundis* and *The Ballad of Reading Gaol* are written anonymously and acclaimed as huge successes. But the poet is incapable of breaking the bonds of Douglas. Deprived of his children (who are forced to change their identity), abandoned by his wife and friends, forsaken and penniless, the King of Life dies quietly and almost anonymously in Paris.

Parandowski began his first sketch, *Antinous,* with the death of Oscar Wilde. The purpose of the sketch was clearly indicated in the epigraph taken from Anatole France, *"Rien n'est vrai que le beau."* *King of Life* begins with a happy childhood and has a chronological sequence. Aside from the above-mentioned investigations of the collision between the ancient and the super-refined modern, Parandowski analyzes the problem of an artist versus society. He shows an amazing perspicacity in dissecting Wilde's milieu. Without moralizing, he exposes; he is somewhat partisan, he idealizes Oscar Wilde. *King of Life* is also something which *Antinous* was not, a brilliant psychological essay. Parandowski is not really interested in creating a detailed biography, although he studied painstakingly the life of Oscar Wilde. He is interested in the study of an image with all its psychological implications.

The study aroused the interest of publishers in Britain, but it
has not yet been translated as Parandowski later recalled:

> Before the war Maria Slomczanka, who lived in Great Britain [and
> who incidentally is still active there, G.H.] translated *The King of
> Life,* and the publishers—in order to avoid possible legal trouble—
> sent the translation to Lord Alfred Douglas. The noble lord sent the
> manuscript back with the remark: "Libel"; the publishers were
> afraid of the risk involved and withdrew from the proposed publi-
> cation. During the war the translation was lost and the translator
> probably died. Now that Lord Alfred is no longer with us, a new
> English translation can be prepared.[1]

King of Life was enthusiastically greeted in Poland and
became a great success. From that time on Parandowski was
recognized as an admirer of antiquity and a brilliant stylist.

CHAPTER 3

Travels and Encounters;
The Olympic Discus

AFTER Poland regained its independence, Warsaw again became the center of cultural as well as political life and attracted a number of writers, artists, critics and scholars. Parandowski decided to leave Lwow, and having found a suitable apartment, moved his family to the capital.

His life there was calm and his literary output considerable. He published several critical essays and extensive reviews on Boleslaw Prus, Jan Kochanowski and Erich Maria Remarque, among others. The two periodicals to which he contributed most often were *Wiadomosci Literackie* (Literary News), for which he had written since 1924, and *Pamietnik Warszawski* (Warsaw Review), a monthly publication founded by the novelist Waclaw Berent. In 1930, with Ludwik H. Morstin, a well-known poet, he became co-editor of *Pamietnik Warszawski*. A number of his articles appeared in it, including several on Anatole France and Flaubert to both of whom he was indebted. Parandowski initiated one of the most important undertakings of this periodical, a series on evolution. He did not retain his co-editorship long. The review was always short of funds and, like many serious publications in Poland, had to rely on financial help from the government. Morstin claimed that it was a quarrel with the representative of the government foundation that moved Parandowski to abandon his co-editorship. Without denying that government interference or curtailment of aid had influenced him, Parandowski said that he lost interest in *Pamietnik Warszawski* and wished to work intensively on his new novel. There is probably some truth in both explanations, for Parandowski refused to meddle in politics.

This is not to say that Parandowski was apolitical or lacked convictions. It was simply that he refused to have his writings

subordinated to the interest of the state. He was a passionate
defender of culture and the personal freedom of a writer. On
many occasions he personally intervened on behalf of writers
and poets. When Wladyslaw Broniewski (1897-1962) was imprisoned for political reasons, it was Parandowski who pleaded
for him and eventually got him released. The state of euphoria
which had overcome not only Parandowski but many other
writers was coming to an end. True, Julian Tuwim, Jan Lechon,
Leopold Staff, Antoni Slonimski and Parandowski still met in
the "Ziemianska" coffee shop, where a special table was reserved
for them and where they discussed poetry and art; but the
country was changing and writers had to take a stand.

Like most Poles, Parandowski was an inveterate traveller.
His primary purpose was to collect material for his work, but
he also travelled to attend congresses, a fashion so charmingly
satirized by Jaroslaw Iwaszkiewicz in his *Congress in Florence*.
Parandowski had more cause to go to such meetings when, at
the end of 1933, he became president of the Polish PEN Club.
His trips as Polish delegate to its international congresses included travelling to Edinburgh in 1934, to Buenos-Aires in
1936 and to Paris in 1937. At these congresses Parandowski
became acquainted with contemporary giants of literature in
many languages—H. G. Wells, Stefan Zweig, James Joyce,
Thomas Mann and Jules Romains among others.

That he deeply valued these associations is demonstrated in
the numerous accounts in his *Odwiedziny i spotkanie* (Visits
and Encounters). After the Paris conference, he wrote a delightful description of a conversation with James Joyce, entitled
"*Spotkanie z Joycem*" (Meeting James Joyce).[1] Much later,
in 1958, in his *Podroze literackie* (Literary Travels), he published a collection of reminiscences of these various encounters.
The work is a blend of memoirs, philosophical reflections and
journalistic reportage. The style varies according to the mood
and the theme, but the collection emerges as an integrated
whole.

The 1930's were tumultuous in Europe; Fascism had a firm
hold on Italy and National Socialism was shortly to overcome
Germany. The PEN meetings were tempestuous indeed. One of
Parandowski's accounts depicting the eleventh congress of the
International PEN is titled *Storm over the Adriatic*. The meeting,

in the old and romantic city of Dubrovnik, resembled the futile sessions of the League of Nations.

There is no doubt where the sympathies of Parandowski lay. It is symptomatic that, when books began to be burned and the first concentration camps to be established, some of the representatives of the West European nations condoned this insanity, or at best were indifferent to it. Typical was a Swiss representative who voted against any condemnation of political persecution, since that would constitute gross interference in the internal affairs of a sovereign state. Parandowski, however, not only condemned the Fascist excesses; he was also an indefatigable promoter of more understanding and closer cultural ties among the non-Fascist nations. He suggested that a Slavic section of the PEN Club be created and Russian writers be included. In view of the almost complete isolation of the Soviet Union at that time, this was a daring proposal.

I　The Olympic Discus

All Greece their boundless praise proclaim.
Teach them, great Jove, with meekness graced
To tread the dazzling paths of Fame,
And Fortune's choicest gifts to taste.

　　　　　　　　　　　　—Pindar

More important was the trip undertaken by Parandowski in 1932 to gather material for a new novel, *Dysk Olimpijski* (The Olympic Discus).[2] Again he was drawn to his beloved Greece; again he yielded to the irresistible fascination this land held for him. In this novel the nature of his interest does not change; it is still the overall life and image of ancient Greece that he seeks to reconstruct. But this general picture serves as the background for one aspect of Greek life on which he focuses special attention: the sport which played such an essential role in this land where the concept of *mens sana in corpore sano* was first developed. In this age, before Christianity had debased the body in order to exalt the soul, physical sport was an integral part of the well-balanced life. Plato was an athlete, as were Euripides and other poets and philosophers.

In order to get the physical perception of the place and to seize what Shakespeare calls "the very age and body of the time," Parandowski travelled to Olympia, an insignificant stop for most tourists. He spent several weeks there, scrupulously measuring everything and recapitulating the physical detail of the stadium. However, all the ruins in Olympia are of a later period than the one Parandowski set out to describe. No remnants of the original detail existed, and he did not want to discuss the reconstructed Olympia.

His research concluded, Parandowski began composing the novel while still in Athens. Instalments were sent as completed to *Tygodnik Illustrowany* (Illustrated Weekly) which serialized the novel in 1932, numbers 1-47, before it appeared in book form in 1933.

Writing in instalments for a periodical is a method of composition which Parandowski has used many times with fruitful results. In conversation with Paul Valéry he stated, and the French poet agreed, that one of the most productive methods of writing is to have a contractual obligation to a newspaper or periodical. Parandowski finds that this generates a pressure and a self-discipline which forces the writer to produce systematically and steadily. We know, of course, that other writers often find this method more burdensome than helpful: one thinks of Dostoyevsky and his bitter struggle to keep one step ahead of his editors.

Parandowski's *Olympic Discus* is divided into two parts, "In the Gymnasium" and "Olympia." The first, as might be expected, depicts the preparation for the Games. Here Parandowski presents the historical background.

The most ancient accounts place the origin of the Olympic Games at the time of Kronos. The first existing historical record dates back to 776 B.C. The event was to take place every five years, later changed to four. It was such an important occurrence in the life of Greece that the time interval of four years between the games was called the Olympiad. At first the program was limited to one day and consisted of one event, a race the length of the stadium; later wrestling, javelin throw, discus throw, chariot races, both of horses and mules, and the pentathlon were added.

A sacred truce was proclaimed by special heralds, *spondoforoi*, first in Elis and then in the rest of Greece, for the duration of the games. The competitors came from all over Greece and its colonies. Barbarians were prohibited from participation. Women were also excluded, not only from the games but from the stadium as well—all save the virgins and priestesses of the goddess Demeter. There were many spectators as well as performers, and the time of the games was used as a congregation for traders, poets and artists.

The solemnities and the ensuing festivities continued for five days, the first part being the time of the competition, the second that of the performance of religious rites and sacrifices. The entire program consisted of twenty-four events, eighteen for adults and six for young boys. As the number of entries grew, the length of the games was extended to seven days. The judges or referees, whose number varied from century to century, were called *hellanodikai.* They directed all the games with the help of a special police force.

Before public appearance, all competitors had to take an oath in front of the statue of Zeus that they had trained for the games ten months, that they were not guilty of any crime, that they would not resort to any trick or ruse, would not accept a bribe, and would uphold the spirit of the Olympic Games. Thirty days before the competition, all participants had to show their skill in the gymnasium before the *hellanodikai.* As a reward the victor was given a wreath made from a branch of a wild olive tree, placed on a bronze tripod, and given palm leaves ·to hold in his hands. This was the greatest honor coveted by and bestowed upon any mortal. Kings competed in the Games alongside commoners. The honors went not only to an individual himself but also to his state or city. There are records showing that aside from fame as national heroes and glorification by the poets, many a winner was able to derive a certain financial gain from his victories. To a Spartan, victory had a particular significance. Plutarch records that efforts were made to bribe a certain Spartan so that he would abstain from the competition. Having rejected the proposal and having won his simple wreath, he was asked what he gained from his victory. "To have the right to fight next to my king," was the proud reply. The skill, the gracefulness, the beauty of the performance were just as esteemed as the victory itself.

The physical setting is all important. Parandowski gives an exact and highly detailed account of the stadium, the sports equipment, and the various events of the Games. The descriptions in *The Olympic Discus* remind the reader of the pictures on ancient Grecian vases.

Parandowski begins his narrative after the proclamation of the truce:

> On an Athenian morning of surpassing freshness the deep tones of the spondophoros' voice echoed with an imposing resonance, breaking the silence that has been spread by the city's trumpeter among the crowds which he had summoned at the first peep of dawn. In the statuelike stillness that supervened, the Agora quadrangle, brightening with the light of day, received the proclamation of a great forthcoming festival.
>
> Olympia was to receive competitors and spectators in the Elean month of Parthenios, at the full of the third moon after the summer solstice. Every free-born Greek undefiled by the taint of homicidal guilt and with no curse of the gods upon his head was eligible by virtue of his civic rights to compete in the Games.[3]

There is then a change in subject, and with it an appropriate modification of style. The author takes his spectators (for this is how one is tempted to call his readers) into the past as he describes the ancient traditions of the Olympic Games with a solemn tone that gives his narrative a somewhat legendary character.

> The time-honored words, rendered still more dignified by the flowing utterance of the Olympic priest, reiterated for the seventy-sixth time the sacred covenant which Iphitos of Elis, Kleisthenes of Pisa, and Lycurgos of Sparta, kings who ruled when the legends were born, had concluded and inscribed upon a bronze disc at the beginning of history. In the memory of the listeners writhed the sharp lettering of the inscription which, resembling a serpent, the divine symbol of eternity, followed a coiled course upon the surface of the circular bronze, from its rim to the center. For three centuries Olympia had called with the same voice. Every fourth year it would intrude between Wrath and Altercation the stadium's gleaming torch.[4]

It was the seventy-sixth Olympiad in the year 476 B.C. which Parandowski set out to describe. Why 476? Because, claimed Parandowski, this Classical period lacked the banality of the

later periods which were depicted in numerous text books,
histories and poems. The previous Festival had been a gloomy
one, marred by the invasion of the Persians and battles which
had left Athens almost in ruins. In the Agora the populace still
remembered it. "It had taken place at the time when Xerxes
crossed the frontiers of Greece—480 B.C.," the time of the last
Olympic Games. Parandowski wanted to show a happy time—
Olympia after the expulsion of the enemy, a time of great expectations, of triumph, of joy and enthusiasm.[5] The forthcoming
Games had all the promise of being an exciting event. The
spondoforoi set out to visit distant lands and inform the people
of the forthcoming events. "The *palaestras* and gymnasiums, as
many as there were throughout the entire extent of the Greek
world, perhaps a thousand, perhaps more, began to stir."[6]

In the next chapter we move back from reminiscence into
reality. As the action begins young athletes arrive and history
acquires flesh and substance. The aspirants undergo all the rigors
of preparation for the Games; the author spares no pains in
giving a full and detailed picture of the gymnasium. Here we
have description of various sports—the broad-jump, wrestling,
discus throwing, javelin throwing, and so one. But most important of all is the glorification of the human body.

Many a critic was at a loss to classify *The Olympic Discus*.
To what genre did it belong? It is hardly appropriate to call it
a novel; it is well-nigh impossible to retell its plot. Yet there is
a unifying idea in the book—a confrontation between two different
attitudes toward the Games: on one hand a detached, professional pragmatism; on the other the idealism of the original
Hellenic concept of sport. There are several vital characters
in the book, among them Sotion, who at once commands our
sympathy and attention. Sotion, because of his physical skill
and strength, is chosen as one of the adult competitors. He and
his friend Sodamos vigorously train for the game. Here we
encounter another problem with psychological as well as social
implications. A new character is introduced—a boy named Ikkos.
He strikes the other participants as singularly queer in his
behavior. To begin with, his eating habits are, in the eyes of the
participants, extravagant. He is not satisfied with their meager
diet of cheese and dry figs, but lets his servant buy him a fish.
His drinking habits are even stranger. The drinking of water

(the only beverage allowed at Olympia) was almost a ritual, and Parandowski devotes considerable space to this important activity.

The donkey-cart carrying the pot-bellied pithos arrived. It had come, driven by an Alean peasant, from the precincts of Akroreia. At dawn he had started downhill from the mountains, reaching here only at noon. He brought fresh water in his well-stoppered earthen jar and was greeted by a burst of cheers on his arrival. Lifting the cover of the jar and filling a goblet, he handed it first to Sodamos, whom he had known the longest. Each in turn tossed aside a small quantity for the gods before drinking, taking care to do this as skillfully as could be managed in order to spill only the fewest drops.[7]

There follows a passage which is a poetical digression on the glorification of water.

Water! The blood of the soil, colorless and pure as the ichor flowing in the veins of the gods! Its sources an unpenetrated secret, it emerges by way of the gravel and stones, pumped onwards, as it were by the rhythmical beat of a heart. In a small fold of the gigantic body of Mother Earth dwells a Naiad, resembling a dewdrop on the coarse bark of an oak. Her whole life's toil is given by this particle of divinity to the uninterrupted spinning of the long-drawn liquid thread, a blessed gossamer. And here is the form of this transparent goddess, the coolness of her virgin beauty, the fragrance of her sylvan hair, the taste of her wet lips; contained in this goblet, all her body—alive and immortal, unadulterated and always the same—enters man.[8]

All this is shaken by the impious and pragmatic approach of Ikkos to water.

The cold draughts were gulped down with a deep sigh and the empty vessel was returned each time with the same unsatisfied avidity. Ikkos in his turn, having received the goblet, did not move but remained lying just as he was and placed the vessel beside himself on the sand. The competitors looked at each other: does he imagine he is lounging at a banquet? With almost a yell Kallias, who was to drink after him, demanded:
"Quicker, others are waiting too!"
Ikkos, seemingly astonished, replied: "Let it warm a bit, it is too cold."
This was beyond belief. The fish, though it still required explanation,

belonged at least to the sphere of human volition in which everybody was free to make his own choice. But to start an argument about water, to accept suspiciously the priceless gift of the gods which on this torrid earth is never abundant—that indeed is real heresy.[9]

The astonishment of the participants grows, for after being understandably irritated by Ikkos's behavior, they discern him to be a sly and methodical youth. It is not the extravagance or individualism in Ikkos which alarms his friends. The athletes sense something wrong but are unable to divine it. Sotion is the one most perturbed, since, like him, Ikkos comes from Tarent. Parandowski puts the two in juxtaposition. Sotion ought to understand Ikkos better, but the men represent two different philosophies, two different attitudes toward the Games. Sotion senses that Ikkos stands for another world. To Sotion the Olympic Games are what their name implies—a game. True enough, they are not to be discarded lightly. They are an integral part of his life. To Ikkos, however, the Games are a cult.

Sotion and Ikkos compete, a physical contest which later on is to acquire cosmic proportions. We do not use the word cosmic lightly; it is Parandowski himself who uses this adjective. Outwardly two individuals are vying for Olympic laurels. Both enter the Games with the idea of competing in the pentathlon. As the rift grows, the reader expects a showdown. The rest of the athletes do not comprehend Ikkos. It is up to Sotion to untangle the web of mystery and riddle. After a few preliminary remarks, Sotion provokes the conversation. Calm and self-possessed as usual, Ikkos answers. Ridiculed because he is too concerned about his health, Ikkos replies that he considers his body an instrument of his trade, of the athlete's profession. Sotion insists that there is no such profession, but Ikkos calmly and convincingly persuades him to the contrary:

If you are offended by the word profession, let us call it an art. I don't suppose that any of you denies that running the pentathlon or wrestling is an art? We are acquiring it, but all have not the same abilities. The days when Glaukos of Karystos could pass straight from the plough to become a boxer have gone.[10]

Sotion is undaunted and persists in his idea, and in his retort finds himself an explanation to Ikkos's behavior.

"But you are overstepping the mark," interrupted Sotion.
"What mark?"
"The Athletic Ideal."
These words fell on them like a radiant beam and all their dislike
for this enigmatic fellow found a dazzling explanation—the truth was
so near that many checked the exclamation of astonishment on their
half-opened lips: how was it that they had not perceived it earlier?[11]

This conversation is, perhaps, the culminating point in the
conflict as Sotion becomes aware of the difference between his
approach to sport and that of Ikkos. To Ikkos's statement, "Our
proficiency is an encouragement and an example," Sotion replies:

"I think so too, but what example can you set to all those who never
diverge from their ordinary life, whom fate does not lead on our
path? Why should you want to give them a body which makes endless
demands and is full of whims? Why drill them into an exaggerated
cautiousness? For what benefit should they surround themselves with
care like a precious statuette in a wooden box? Really, one would
imagine they were fragile things liable to be shattered or damaged."
"And what would you have them do?"
"Nothing, I would leave them where they are in those gardens of
gaiety and freedom, the *palaestras* and gymnasiums which our an-
cestors built through the favor of the gods. I am one of those too,
only I differ from them in that a happy fate allowed me to proceed
to Olympia—a happy fate, nothing else."[12]

"Happy fate" brought Sotion to Olympia; Sotion the ephebe,
"vowed to no aim and singularly unencumbered," who "shone
like a strayed fragment of the Golden Age giving out the gleam
of his happy and purposeless life." This then is the explanation
and the leitmotiv of the book. A symbolic picture ends the first
part as a friend rushes up and bears the athlete on his shoulders
through the cheering throng. "Sotion slung his leg on the giant's
shoulder, clambered up and sat astride his neck, like a young
Dionysos riding on a hairy Seilenos."[13]

The second part of the book begins again with a digression
about the Greek world, stretching from Scythia to Egypt, and
then returns to Olympia. The crowds arrive, and finally, after
several processions and ceremonies, competition begins. On the
second day the Games open at the Hippodrome. There are

several horse races, and their description is every bit as exciting as that of any modern race. Beauty and suspense abound. Ikkos breaks the regulations by training in a stadium, which is strictly forbidden. Sotion surprises him but does not betray him. Then follows the pentathlon, one of the most graceful competitions. "It produced the best built men, the cream of pentathletes." Here is a description of unsurpassed plasticity:

The sight of these bodies was comparable to everything that gives the quintessence of joy. It could be compared with a starry night, for in addition to their palpable sensual splendor there was in them the deep meaning that attaches to perfect things.[14]

The most handsome, most graceful, is Sotion himself, whose body transcends the limits of the physical and acquires a deeper meaning.

His physique, the rounded shapeliness of his head and neck, the delicate lips, the straight nose, the hair which in the sun appeared to be still lighter, the expressive eyes—the whole was of the purest Hellenic blood; the very soul of the race, it seemed, had embodied itself in this youth.[15]

Now comes the culminating point of *The Olympic Discus.* Three quoits are brought in and the competitors take their chance at them. It is a solemn moment. The quoits are old, as old as the original discus with the inscription. The depiction of the throw, of unbelievable plasticity and motion, is the high point of the book. It is Myron's sculpture coming to life:

He thrust the right leg forward and, though the weight of the body was supported on the left leg, the right, with its tense calf muscles, and the firmly planted foot were ready to uphold his action. He resorted to it the next moment, when passing the discus from the left to the right hand. He bent forwards, then sharply turned to the right—his whole frame twisted, a living prefiguration of Myron's bronze—and straightened up again, shifting the weight of the body on to the right leg. Then, for the last time, he stepped back; his arm made three swings like a pendulum—a grand lever of tendons and muscle—and, finally discharged the discus.
It flew level, cutting the air noiselessly, one could have taken it for a streak of fire, and when it descended it bounded up with a

ring—once, twice, thus in a mortal paroxysm parting with its soul,
its content of eternal motion.

After the throw Sotion remained with arms outspread and poised
upon the muscles of his right leg. His lungs were full of breath, until
a sonorous impulsive shout burst from them when the discus passed
Ikkos's mark.[16]

And yet Sotion does not win the pentathlon. The last event
is the competition in wrestling, and it is the sly, methodical
Ikkos who wins. The exuberance of Sotion is too honest; competition for him is pure joy and nothing else. That same after-
noon he is the loneliest man on earth, for the crowd of spectators
turns away from him.

In *The Olympic Discus* Parandowski's most important achievement is doubtless his superb description of the physical appearance as well as the motion of the human body. Several examples
have been given, but one more should be mentioned. It is a
portrait of a young girl, all the more striking since there are no
women in this all-male society. Her character is not developed
in *The Olympic Discus,* but here are the classical lines of her
appearance:

The scanty Dorian peplos did not hide the lines of her body nor
smother her figure in a superabundance of drapery. The young bloom
of her shapely curves could be gauged through this piece of cloth
which, gathered at the waist, hung in long parallel folds. Every pace
threw these pleats open and beneath the soft wool a glimpse of the
full and perfect leg was revealed. Broad in the shoulders, with bold
breasts that swelled under the apoptygma covering them, the slender-
ness of her arms, her neck and her feet peeping from their sandals
announced to the world that her body was nourished by the sun of
the coasts and the wind of the sea.[17]

Hydna is drawn to Sotion, but there is no love motive in the
book. There is a gentle hint and insinuation of it, but otherwise
Hydna admires Sotion's beauty just as any other athlete would.

In Parandowski's writings on antiquity we have already
observed his fondness for projection from the past to modern
times and back again. This tendency, noticeable in *The Two
Springs* and in *King of Life,* is also present in *The Olympic
Discus.* Its epilogue is a cursory description of the subsequent

development of the Olympic Games. Sport loses its former
dignity and splendor. Athletics become a spectacle for spectators: no longer is there an athletic ideal. The ideas of Ikkos
triumph. The development and the decadence of Olympian
sport has a striking similarity to some developments in modern
times. The athletes are pampered and groomed with the greatest
of care, their diets, weights, and habits watched. No longer is
it requisite to be Greek to participate in the sports. Olympic
Games become, to use the modern term, big business.

Reading the epilogue, one is involuntarily reminded of Anatole
France, and particularly of the conclusion of *Penguin Island*
with its mild skepticism about our civilization. *The Olympic
Discus* ends on a nostalgic note. Olympia undergoes a change:
it is covered with sleet, it is destroyed, its inhabitants are scattered to the four winds. But at the end of the nineteenth
century come the archeologists and later, modern Olympic
Games are re-established. "The spirit of Greek agonistics began
its second life, to repeat once more all former virtues and errors."

This, then, is Parandowski's *Olympic Discus*. He will continue
his study of antiquity in *Trzy znaki zodiaku* (The Three Signs
of the Zodiac) and *Godzina srodziemnomorska* (The Mediterranean Hour), both collections much more loosely constructed
than *The Olympic Discus*. In each one he takes one single
incident in Greek history, but by giving it a historical background, creates a wider canvas of Greek life. *The Olympic
Discus* became highly popular in Poland, read by adults and
students alike. The author stated that he took the names of his
heroes from Pindar and from various writers of Byzantium.
By introducing the historical figures the books acquire greater
reality. Homer's verses are quoted and mentioned incessantly
by the characters in the book. Pindar is often mentioned and
Themistocles arrives at the Games.

An interesting incident occurred after the Second World War
when Parandowski visited one of the high schools where passages of *The Olympic Discus* were required reading. When
Parandowski was introduced by the teacher to the students, they
thought he was joking; in front of them stood a kindly, middle-
aged man, gentle and of average height. They could not understand how a man who was not a giant with bulging muscles

could describe the sports events with such insight and perspicacity.

At the Olympic Games in Berlin in 1936, over the protests of the Germans, Parandowski was awarded a bronze medal for *The Olympic Discus*. This book also introduced Parandowski to West-European readers, his first major work to be translated into several languages. Preparations were made to have it translated into German. The translation was duly made and a German firm, Gurlitt, was to publish it. In 1939 the entire edition was ordered destroyed. The translator died during the German occupation of Poland, and the publishing house was bombed out during the war.[18] It was only after the war that the German translation of *The Olympic Discus* was published, first in Switzerland, then in the German Democratic Republic, and finally in the Federal Republic of Germany. As if by coincidence, the book appeared in English in London in September of 1939, a month so memorable to all Poles. Parandowski knew nothing of it until a friend sent word to him through a Polish patriot, dropped by parachute into Poland.

The writer, fighting then for a bare existence, hardly gave this translation a second thought. However, in 1946 at the first postwar PEN Congress in Stockholm, he told this adventure to Margaret Storm Jameson, who was greatly surprised that the author had had no chance to see his work in translation and promised her good offices to obtain a copy for him. Shortly after, Parandowski, who had lingered in Sweden, received a note from Miss Jameson that no copies of *The Olympic Discus* were available and that the publishing house from which it had appeared existed no longer. There remained only one way to obtain a copy: to write to *The Times* and appeal to Parandowski's readers. To his great delight, several copies were sent to him. Letters came not only from Britain but from other countries of the British Commonwealth as well. "It was delightful," wrote Parandowski later, "to realize that in those trying days, under the German occupation, this book had access to distant houses of strangers and possessed freedom of which I could not even dare to dream."[19]

Further evidence of his growing international reputation is the fact that this English translation was republished by Ungar in New York in 1964, with a new preface by the present writer.

CHAPTER 4

Heaven in Flames

". . . ils pleurent d'avoir perdu ce
qu'ils ne possédaient pas."

—*Toepffer*

FATHERLAND is an abstraction, Parandowski wrote at one
time. If it were to take form in one's imagination, it would
have to take concrete shape or appear as a symbol. At the sound
of this word some people see a map of the country or its flag,
and others remember some countryside, its fields and rivers, a
village or some city. Parandowski belongs to the second group.
He is much attached to Warsaw, but the city in his memory and
imagination does not exist alone; around it whirls a small rural
satellite by the name of Swider. The writer and his family spent
many days and weeks in this modest countryside at the hotel
"Sloneczna." Many hours of creative work were spent there. It
was in Swider that Parandowski heard the first rumbling of
the war.

One evening, the writer recalls, he told his wife that he had
an idea for a new novel on a topic hardly touched upon in
Polish literature—a religious crisis in the soul of a young boy.
Again, as with *The Olympic Discus*, the author was drawn by
the novelty of the subject matter. Noteworthy is the fact that
the idea occurred to Parandowski right after the completion
of his previous novel. Apparently once thrown into the literary
and creative cyclotron the writer's mind could not hold back
its creative processes. Whatever the reason, 1934-35 is marked
by very fertile and prolific literary and journalistic activity.

In selecting a setting as the background for his psychological
study Parandowski decided to place his hero in that part of the
country which the author knew best—his native Lwow. The
action takes place at the time of Parandowski's own childhood.

53

Childhood impressions are of course the most lasting, hence many writers attempt to return to their formative years. This is not to say that they necessarily depict childhood experiences. This fact should be stressed because before Parandowski's novel appeared in book form (it was serialized in *Gazeta Polska*), it was subjected to a great deal of criticism and a heated controversy surrounded it. Many critics took it for granted that Parandowski was depicting his own childhood. The misunderstanding was supported by the fact that the main character, Teofil Grodzicki, bore the name of Parandowski's grandmother. After the war, in a new 1956 edition, the writer tried to explain to what extent his *Niebo w plomieniach* (Heaven in Flames) was an autobiographical novel.

We know that no writer works in a vacuum; willy-nilly he incorporates many of his impressions and interpretations of the world around him in his work. A striking example, illustrating the extent to which childhood experiences can be utilized in a novel without turning the work into an autobiography, is the case of Tolstoy. It is well-known that Tolstoy's diary served as the raw material for his earlier works, particularly for his "autobiographical trilogy," yet no one nowadays would claim that Nikolenka was meant to be the young Tolstoy. Parandowski's Teofil is a fictional character, as Nikolenka is, but both characters are an integral part of their respective creators. A number of incidents involving Teofil were invented to show his developing character and he was surrounded by a number of fictional characters, in order to unfold his personality.

There is no reason to suggest that Parandowski followed Tolstoy's example, although there are several incidents in the novel which are similar to incidents in the trilogy. Both authors depict similar experiences; Tolstoy's hero is a self-analytical boy and the narrative is kept within the first person pattern, at times almost becoming a memoir. Parandowski's work remains a novel and is kept within the boundaries of this genre.

The author limits his description of society to one class only—that of the officials. The rest of the personages, with the exception of the high school teachers, are incidental and have the role of an auxiliary cast, for an attempt to give a more general, wider picture of the city and its society would necessarily

overwhelm the main character and push him into the background.

Closely connected with the hero's religious problem is the
conflict which develops between father and son. This conflict
makes another problem evident, that of his relationship with
the church, or to be more exact, the collision between the hero
and the church's representatives.

Teofil, a precocious and sensitive child, through his own
searchings and by a coincidence (a friend of his gives him
Renan's *Life of Jesus* to read), loses his faith. The loss of
religious belief necessitates a search and confirmation. Teofil
reads avidly to find some substitute for his faith. He finds it
in the Theory of Evolution and in science. Teofil is not satisfied
with silent reflection; he feels an inner need to talk, and becomes
a propagandist of his new negative belief.

One day when he holds a discussion on religion in the park,
Teofil is overheard by a priest from his school. The eavesdropping has far-reaching consequences for young Grodzicki. Father
Grozd denounces him, and over the pupil's head hangs the
threat of expulsion from the school. Rojek, the Greek teacher,
a downtrodden failure maltreated by his wife, warns Teofil's
father of the impending disaster. He does so because he feels
that the punishment meted out to Teofil would be too harsh,
and because Grodzicki was his old school friend. Grodzicki
boldly goes to the principal of the school, talks to him and to
the priest and removes the danger. A secret deal is concluded
at this "Vanity Fair": Grodzicki promises his good offices to
help Grozd obtain a position soon to be vacant at the cathedral.

Here the second conflict begins, between the boy and his
father who struggles to rescue his son from atheism. Meanwhile,
Teofil undergoes further crises aggravated by the death of one
of his school friends. A question looms before him; if there is
no afterlife, what then? The dying friend himself raises the
question stating that atheism is for strong individuals only.
After the death Teofil becomes bitter because of his lack of
faith. The conflict is never resolved and it is doubtful that it
could have been. Teofil is not a very positive character; at times
he shows the pusillanimity of a "superfluous" man. As one old
teacher, Kalina, says, "Nine boys out of ten go through the

same crisis, but overcome it." Teofil's conflict is more serious and lasting; and this is the essence of the novel.

The book ends with the Grodzickis' trip to Abazzia on the very eve of World War I. The end is symbolic, almost like the final episode in Zola's *La bête humaine* except that the reader has no macabre premonitions but feels that his heroes will be saved from imminent disaster. As the train moves along, the sleeping Teofil has a dream in which his friend Jurkin beckons to him leaning on a rifle, and he wears a uniform unknown to Grodzicki: Polish independence is not far off. The timekeeper lingers over Teofil, full of anxiety, expectations and hope.

The novel, a realistic one, reveals Teofil as a cerebral being rather than a physical. We know little about his appearance except for the fact that he was a handsome boy of average build and strength. As the author prepares him systematically for the coming conflict, his mental struggles predominate. Teofil's character is revealed by his reaction to things and to people, and in this Parandowski is a master. Like Tolstoy's hero, Teofil wakes up and the exposition of his spiritual and mental being begins.

Conflict starts, on a small scale, in the first pages when the father rebukes his son for bad school marks. An oblique allusion to this conflict is suggested by the precise and detailed description, worthy of Balzac, of the orderly and meticulous flat. The furniture and that good old fetish, the clock, point to the solidity and continuity of the family. It is as if this orderly life and family stability were threatened by the boy's departure from traditional religious beliefs. A suggestion of a conflict between father and son is also contained in the description of the father's desk, filled with all kinds of small things enticing to the child. Teofil always wanted to penetrate the mysteries of its contents, but the thought of it somehow was always connected with the thought of the father's death.

We must admire Parandowski's carefully controlled and gradual development of the conflict theme, as it proceeds from minor matters to the major issues of the novel. For example, Teofil has some trouble with Latin, which brings him into conflict with his teachers. When Teofil tells his father about it, he retorts that learning opens the door to many careers, but that one nevertheless does not have to believe in everything the teachers tell. The teachings of our Holy Church are the only ones which one has to obey.

Yet another theme is introduced when the author depicts the boy's sexual awakening. Teofil is shy, but when he meets some young girls he feels the need for a brushing and is ashamed of his clothes. Passing a sculpture of a nude, a scandal among the city fathers, Teofil avoids looking at its face but peeps furtively at the legs, the hips, and the bosom.

Parandowski ends this chapter with an allusion to the next incident: after seeing the sculpture Teofil meets a young girl. His father has a birthday and a number of guests arrive, among them Alina, who later on will be the subject of erotic aspirations. As the guests entertain themselves Teofil sees himself as some sort of desperado who orders all the men to be put in chains and all the women stripped naked and brought before him. With his usual irony Parandowski remarks that if somebody had guessed Teofil's thoughts and asked him what he intended to do after the stripping, the young boy would have difficulty in answering the question. The first erotic sensation follows. Alina and Teofil play "post office" in a dark room and exchange their first kiss. At confession Teofil tells the priest that he kissed a girl and wants to see her again. The priest, modest and kind, whose very name "Skromny" signifies humility, is touched by the innocence of the confession and instead of absolving him with a few religious platitudes, silently makes over him the sign of the cross.

The author shows Teofil as an individual deeply rooted in religion and Catholic tradition. The conflict and the collision which ensue are all the more striking and convincing. If some critics saw in the novel total abnegation of the church, they were mistaken. The author shows the quest of the young boy and presents a very unattractive priest, selfish and cunning, but then there are several positive characters among the clergy. Furthermore, the father's efforts to woo his son are described with great sympathy, even if he does not always succeed in winning his arguments. It would therefore be wrong to assume that Parandowski is anti-Catholic. Quite the contrary, for the novel contains a hidden apologia for the church.

Symbolically, Teofil's religious conflict begins at Easter time, when the boy reads Renan's *Life of Jesus*. Though the book makes an unpleasant impression on him, he studies it attentively. He becomes obsessed with religion, he does not notice anything around him, his erotic development is arrested and he no longer notices Alina. Teofil tells his mother about his loss of faith, but neither she nor the priest Skromny, in whom Teofil confides, understand him. The priest thinks it a passing experience not to be tampered with.

Teofil's doubts grow, however, as his investigations reveal contradictions in the Christian Church. He reads the Apocrypha, learns about the god Mithra whose birthday coincides with that of Christ. Teofil sees the parallel between the flight to Egypt and the flight of the Egyptian Hathor with the little Horos. When the Hindu Krishna was born, the wicked king Kamsa ordered the massacre of all small children: the parallel to the biblical legend is again compelling. Teofil's search leads him to search into the history of the church; he reads Joseph Flavius and the Fathers of the Church but cannot reconcile what he reads with the frailties of the representatives of the cult. Here the crisis reaches its high point: during a thunderstorm the boy runs home hurling defiance to the Heavens. To Teofil's inquietude, Parandowski juxtaposes the calm faith of his mother and father. Seeing her son in great agitation his mother involuntarily makes the sign of the cross.

Teofil's adversary, the priest Grozd, is depicted in the blackest possible colors, as greedy, sly, lying, hypocritical. His passion for collecting picture frames makes him ridiculous. Grozd is intelligent, yet a fanatic; even Teofil's father thinks that had Grozd lived at the time of the Inquisition he would have been the most ruthless executioner of heretics.

Grodzicki accepts Christianity in the lateral sense but with a touch of pagan pantheism: he believes that he came from the earth and will go back to it. How could it be otherwise when the earth gives such a magnificent bounty? The market scene in which the father makes peace between life and death is the most poignant and magnificent passage in the novel. Moving about among the abundance of agricultural produce, the father remarks that here is the meaning of life. He is a high official but basically a peasant in his perception of the universe: hence his reflection, *"Beatus ille, qui procul negotiis paterna rura bubus exercet suis . . ."* (Happy is the one who, free from public duties, plows the ancestral fields with his oxen.) Emperor Diocletian left his power and his throne to cultivate cabbage. What is as intricate as a wheat ear? How could anything as profound as the Words "Give us our daily bread" be imagined? The elemental perception, barbaric and pagan at the same time, merges into unsophisticated Christian belief.

Thus the novel presents us with several different types of religious belief. Orthodox Catholicism, Teofil's anguished agnosticism and the father's pantheistic Catholicism which is shared by Prussota, who likewise has a cosmic perception of God. To Prussota, a country priest whose very name suggests early Polish Christianity, God is an indefatigable creator. From early in the morning till late at night his gray-haired God toils, taking a break to wash His hands, singed by some distant star. The deeds and the words of this giant make an indelible impression upon Teofil; he is profoundly moved by this Christian vision, and the text of the Apocrypha, full of pantheistic significance, resounds in his ears: "Lift up a stone and you will find me there, split up a tree and there also am I."

Though an Austrian official, Grodzicki is first a Polish patriot, just as Prussota's image, one of the most profound and meaningful, is symbolic of Polish history. The conflict between father and son is never resolved. The father, unable to convince his son, is afraid to become ridiculous in his eyes and abandons his books and his arguments. Time moves on, life dictates its own laws, and Teofil's aloofness is shattered. His quest and searching are replaced by a new passion. As the boy grows up, his words and thoughts turn to the subject common to all young boys: women. Gone are the days when their words fell on his deaf ears and he was impervious to their conversations. Alina shakes him out of his lethargy.

In contrast to Teofil, a cerebral type, Alina is an elemental and direct personality. Hardly would she worry about religion; she is convinced the church would sanctify her love. Parandowski confronts Teofil, the reflecting personality, with Alina, the earthiest of all characters. It is not so much what she thinks, but what she feels that counts. To Alina, being a woman is like being the earth, blooming and giving birth to great bounty. The earth is like a girl, modest in the spring, then becoming enticing and exciting, with a golden body, an arid fragrance, and shame-

less loud laughter. Science and learning do not interest Alina;
it is only Teofil she desires. "What would we do Alina," Teofil
asks her one day, "if we were the first people on earth?" The
answer is unequivocal: "The same as those. I would pick an
apple, you would eat it and we would find out that we are
naked." It is the earth which draws Teofil back to life and it
is Alina with her charm who triumphs.

I *Style and Technique*

Heaven in Flames is a relatively short novel, consisting of
twenty-six brief chapters, which unfold in strict chronological
sequence. This direct technique is obviously the most effective
and logical way to depict the development of Teofil through his
formative years. Upon closer investigation, however, the reader
will see that the simplicity of style and organization is deceptive.
The novel, which at first glance appears to be written in the
conventional realistic style of the nineteenth and early twentieth
centuries, is a complex entity. The work is clear and concise,
so concise that each chapter, each sentence and each detail is
indispensable—to remove any of it would be to run the risk of
destroying the construction of its logical unity.

The author begins his novel without any preliminaries, plung-
ing the reader into the midst of the action. He introduces his
personages but does not unduly explain their characters; most
of the time he lets his heroes speak and think aloud. The chapters
are interconnected, each one usually ending with an allusion
to the action in the next. The narrative acquires a certain rhythm,
and each chapter concludes with a *cul-de-lampe*, a vignette.

In the first chapter the reader discovers the main character,
with his school problems; his mother, a calm and detached
person who is an intermediary between father and son; and
finally the father himself, a man of humble origin, conservative
but kind and thoughtful, who has made a brilliant career as a
high official in the provincial government. Parandowski makes
Grodzicki reveal his past by reading the family chronicle, to
which he adds a piece every evening. Every morning, at the
breakfast table, he reads the event recorded for that particular
day for the preceding year. This retrospection unfolds the
history of the family for twelve years, reveals the father as a
man, and at the same time makes the reader aware that all this

happened on the eve of World War I. The chronicles of the
twelve days of the twelve consecutive years briefly permit an
insight into the world political situation. The first item deals with
the Boer War at the same time that the mother muses that she
is perturbed and could not sleep for thinking about a Russian
reconnaissance plane allegedly making frequent flights over the
city. Listening to the father's reading of the chronicle, all the
participants are moved by its charm and simplicity and remember
the years gone by. Thus the author completes the background of
each member of the family. This fenestration device and the
projection into the past is characteristic of Parandowski's literary
technique. The narrative acquires new substance, the picture
becomes wider, the characters become sharply delineated.

Another device used to broaden the narrative is the walk. The
characters walk a great deal. The element of motion and of
progression is important; each walk has a certain significance.
Teofil has an assignment for his school work—the historical
monuments of the city; he takes a walk and the writer creates
a real background. The city of Lwow comes to life, its past
being recapitulated. Rojek, the teacher who had warned Teofil's
father of the boy's trouble, walks to school and sees Teofil. He is
afraid of the boy and goes to the other side of the street. Here
the author digresses into Rojek's past, his friendship with
Grodzicki and his resentment of Grodzicki's success, which is
the reason he dislikes Teofil. Walking from the faculty meeting
at which Teofil was discussed, Rojek stops at Grodzicki's. This
marks a turning point in his relationship to Teofil.

Father Grozd also takes walks, for reasons of health, and on
one of his walks he overhears Teofil's conversation with the
boys. The most perfect example of how the narrative motion
blends with the spiritual or the intellectual issues is given by
the author in the conversation that follows between Dr. Kos
and Father Grozd. Eavesdropping, Father Grozd in turn is
surprised by Kos. After the boys disperse, the two walk on and
converse. Walking and talking become two inseparable elements.
Teofil constantly moves around, be it in the city or in the
country; the parents too walk or drive around. The market
scene, one of the salient points in the novel, is full of motion.
Rojek's undoing happens as he walks along the street and
decides to drop into a tavern for a drink. Grozd, walking behind

him, sees him and denounces him as a drunk. Teofil discovers
Father Prussota on one of his walks in the country. This passage
is one of the most lyrical in the novel.

As so often happens in Parandowski's work, the physical and
the spiritual form an inseparable whole: they merge, and a
number of objects have a symbolic significance. In the beginning of the book it was the clock and at the end it is an electric
light bulb.

Heaven in Flames is a novel which is symmetrically constructed. The author achieves symmetry through the well-known
device of juxtaposition. If we speak about the physical setting,
there are two parts in the novel. Two apartments are described,
and it is in the second, into which the family moves over the
mother's protestations, that the electricity is installed. The bulb
becomes a physical symbol of progress; Teofil compares the
installation of the bulb to the changing of certain philosophical
ideas. The first apartment was the residence of a well-established
family, set and sedate; the family moves into the second flat
when the father achieves a certain station in life, promoted to
the rank and title of *Hofrat* (court counselor). The juxtaposition
of ideas embodied in two buildings is contained in the comparison between the governor's palace and the Church of the
Carmelites. Taking a walk, the father—a dual personality of a
family man and a civil servant—points out the difference to
his wife:

Two worlds, temporal and eternal, stood next to each other in glaring
contrast.

The stern block of the Governor's office building, the gloomy
darkness of which was not disturbed by a single lighted window,
cumbered the ground, sealed with close fitting pavement slabs
which resounded with the measured step of a sentry. It was evident
that the spirit of these walls took space and time seriously and
expected that they too would treat it with respect. The black double-
headed eagle on a yellow shield did not make it more graceful;
burdened by the golden apple and the sword it renounced flight and
wanted to remain eternally on the land which it had grabbed and
plundered a hundred years ago.

The church on the other hand, slighted the earth, which pursued
it with the staircases and terraces and with the entire enraptured
height of the trees, the crowns of which dreamt to reach the Cross
one day.[1]

The conflict between father and son runs through the whole novel. There are, moreover, a number of other characters juxtaposed in the work who are carriers of various ideas and ideologies. To begin with, there are several priests in the novel. Skromny, a kind and somewhat innocuous man, is contrasted with Father Grozd, ambitious and viciously dogmatic, but an intelligent servant of the church. Father Prussota is a pioneer, a peasants' priest who lacks the subtleties of Grozd.

The teachers also differ from each other. Dr. Kos is a free-thinker, but a man incapable of any concrete action, similar to a hero of Sienkiewicz's *Bez dogmatu* (Without Dogma) and also similar to a number of Russian "superfluous" people who are characterized, to borrow the expression of Sienkiewicz, by "l'improductivité slave." Kos has a number of projects in mind but he is unable to implement them either in education or in life. What makes him so different from other similar characters of nineteenth century literature is that in everyday life he is a cautious and practical man. He is unwilling to come to Teofil's rescue, and shuns him at the time of his conflict. Opposed to Dr. Kos is Rojek who first dislikes Teofil because he envies the success of Teofil's father, but who offers a helping hand to the young boy, an action which ultimately proves to be detrimental to his own career.

Noteworthy also is the sequence of events in the novel, which follows in many ways the awakening of the hero. The physical awakening mentioned in the first page suggests the spiritual awakening and the emergence of a quest. The novel is a sequence of days and nights; many chapters begin with "Teofil woke up" or "Teofil woke up with a disturbing feeling of guilt" (Chapter I), "Teofil woke up in the middle of the night" (Chapter VII), or "after the communion Teofil lived through a difficult night" (Chapter IX). With the development of the conflict Teofil becomes exhausted, and "closes his eyes and falls asleep" (Chapter XIII). In the same chapter Teofil resumes contact with reality, and his conflict is overshadowed by the interest in Alina: "Teofil woke up at the sound of a voice, which seemed to belong to his sleep. However it was a real voice. Alina went by, accompanied by a young man." And finally the novel is concluded with Teofil's sleep and his symbolic vision. The reader does not see his next awakening.

Parandowski in his *Heaven in Flames* is a master of dialogue, through which he constantly reveals the character of his heroes. Because the principal idea of the book is psychological and ethical, the role of discussion, conversation, or musing, is of paramount importance. The inner conflict of Teofil is revealed through his inner dialectic. Several types of conversation are discernible in the work; dialogue, inner monologue and even inner dialogue. All characters in the novel are actively engaged in discussions, ranging from everyday communications to philosophical discourse and to diplomatic pirouettes between Grodzicki the father, Father Grozd and Zubrzycki, the principal of the high school.

Each character uses his own vocabulary; his mode of expression is highly individualized. Grodzicki's pronouncements are first calm and benevolent, becoming vexed and agitated later in the conflict. Unforgettable are the lines describing the scene in which the father goes to speak to the principal. Here it is not what is said that is important, but what is left unsaid. They play a clever diplomatic game, and Parandowski displays a deep dramatic talent. The dialogue changes when Grodzicki confronts his astute opponent, Father Grozd. Carefully, each maneuvers the other into a deal; the words and speech are full of subtle hints and equivocations kept within the framework of a relationship between a clergyman and a layman. In contrast, Teofil's mother, serving as an intermediary in the conflict and the dispute, has a conciliatory and simple tone of voice. Dr. Kos is logical and articulate; he enjoys talking and at times like Father Grozd, he is enraptured with his own speech. Father Grozd's language betrays a man of self-assurance and self-righteousness. He, too, is steeped in a game of sophistry. Kalina stands somewhat apart from the rest of the characters; he does not argue. A man of great erudition and intellectual integrity, he preaches and lectures to Teofil.

The silent and lonely Rojek becomes loquacious after his talk with Teofil's father. This, we remember, was the turning point in the relationship between Rojek and Teofil. A certain rapport is established between the two in the classroom. A good example of an inner dialogue is contained in the mute conversation between the old Greek teacher and Teofil. This is how the author depicts the silent communication:

On that empty waste, which was the Greek lesson, the thoughts of the pupil and the teacher met and greeted each other from afar:

"Who are you, you old crank, who comes at night to disrupt the peace of the house and protect it from further disturbances?"

"Who are you, my boy, who struggled with God and brings the lonely ones under the roof of his friends?"

"Do I have to value in you something more than the youth of my father, of which you are a memory?"

"You misty phantom, born on the day when my son left me forever, did you encounter him on the way down to earth?"

Thus conversed two hearts over the insect-like humming of the classroom amidst the crackling of Greek words bursting like nutshells, revealing their pithy flesh from under the suffixes, conjunctions and augments.[2]

Rojek is a pedagogue able to arouse the interest of his pupils in Greek culture. Parandowski here yields to the temptation to come back to his beloved subject, Antiquity. The pages depicting the upsurge of Teofil's curiosity about the Greek language may well describe the author's own experiences. As Teofil studies the language, the process becomes a game: he collects words as he would collect postage stamps. The game, however, acquires more serious meaning when Teofil, groping in Greek culture, attains a deeper comprehension of the language. The pupil and the teacher achieve perfect harmony in a classroom:

How many feelings could be expressed by the affirmative nod of the head, how eloquent were the wrinkles around the eyes. What rich gesture it was when the hand suddenly was lifted and the fingertips glided over the mustache.

These silent signs, recognitions which the teacher bestowed upon him for his answers, were to Teofil dearer than any formal recognition. At times a short dispute developed. Rubbing his bald head violently, Rojek repeated with a drawn-out voice the same word, as if conjuring its spirit which did not want to reveal itself. Teofil cast one word after another, each becoming closer and more exact until finally he found the only one fitting the atmosphere of the Greek idea. For a couple of seconds the pupil and the teacher remained gripped by a silent emotion as if a brilliant meteor flashed above them.[3]

In Teofil's face, Rojek sees his own son come to life, resurrected. Father Grozd, in contrast, forgets altogether what his pupil looks like, finding it more interesting to dream about the position he covets in the cathedral and to spend his time seeking out useful quotations from the Bible.

The Greek teacher's enthusiasm is important for Teofil's intellectual and ethical development. From a purely aesthetic problem, the culture of Ancient Greece, he moves to its religion; Rojek becomes an hierophant for his pupils: after his lectures a pagan smoke billows in the classroom. Teofil's friends confront the young boy with a question of the validity and superiority of monotheism over polytheism. Teofil defends polytheism. The author, a professed Catholic, juxtaposes two worlds in his novel, a Christian and a pagan, to give a new impetus to Teofil's religious quest. The problem of monotheism versus polytheism must have been important for Parandowski; in *Heaven in Flames* Teofil voices the opinions and doubts of the author, who touches upon this question on several occasions.

The theme is particularly prominent in a collection called *The Mediterranean Hour*. In one of the sketches, "Roscher," published in 1949, the author shows that he has gone through an evolution in his religious thinking. Deeply rooted in the culture of antiquity, he is fascinated by its religion. Almost all the elements are identical in the chapter of *Heaven in Flames* and in the sketch: the evolution of Japanese culture, the wisdom of the ancients, the perplexing question. Teofil's passionate if subdued retort in defense of polytheism, "Could any of the Grecian gods spill the blood of thousands of people for just one word or one syllable!" is re-echoed in the latter, more somber, "Roscher":

One day I hope to read a study of Greek religion written by a Japanese. I think it would differ widely from our own studies and perhaps would be far more valuable—provided the author resisted the influence of European scholarship. For what handicaps us most in this field is monotheistic education; as a matter of fact none of us understands paganisms and all our commentaries are nothing but an illusory cover for ignorance. Only a man to whom the world, since his early childhood, has been the creation and seat of many gods, and who, for his part, suspects in all opinions that the opposite is true, is capable of understanding every variety of polytheism, alien as it may be to him in race and epoch. How many scholars, whose services to Greek mythology are still remembered with admiration,

were absolutely helpless in this field! They were like people lost in
a forest, vainly trying to find their way, though they knew the name,
height and age of every tree. Monotheism made them lose their
bearings and many of them arranged their histories of gods in camou-
flaged monotheistic systems.

It is not by accident that I have mentioned a Japanese. For I
once knew such a one, who has perhaps by now fulfilled a long-
standing need and written such a book. He sat down beside me on
the stairway of the Syracusan treasury in Olympia when, among the
ruins of the stadium, I was tracing the shadow of my Sotion. He was
a student at the Sorbonne, a philologist. We talked for several hours
and it was he—a polytheist by birth and conviction—who was so
mockingly critical of the European approach to the history of religion.
But while I was able to grasp and memorize his criticism, his lectures
on the proper meaning of polytheism did not take hold of my imagination and memory: I listened to them as if to an initiation into the
mysteries, but the words failed to strike root in my Christian mind.

What made him most indignant was the view that monotheism
was a superior form of religion and that any justification at all was
needed for the fact that people as intelligent as the old Athenians,
or as sensible as the Romans, should have thought that polytheism was
true and accepted the bewildering confusion of Myths.[4]

But let us return to the novel; one of its characteristics is the
author's all-pervading humor. Almost all of the characters, and
all of the situations, are treated with gentle irony and detached
skepticism. The sole exception is Teofil himself; he is too intent
and too wrapped up in his conflict. The author also restrains his
irony when he describes a lyrical or deeply emotional situation.

Parandowski's irony stems from several sources: it can be
traced as far back as Greek and Roman writers; it reflects the
eighteenth-century ironic skepticism of the Enlightenment and,
finally, twentieth-century skepticism, particularly that of Anatole
France.

In one of his chapters Parandowski describes a card game
in the house of Grodzicki in which Father Grozd participates.
Grodzicki tells the company that the game they are playing is
called l'abbé. Invented in the eighteenth century, it was popular
in certain circles of worldly priests who, says the father, are
depicted in contemporary engravings and pictures surrounded
by a bevy of beautiful women dressed in exceptionally low-cut
gowns. In this dialogue between Father Grozd and Grodzicki,

French encyclopedists are mentioned and Voltaire's famous irony is alluded to. If Voltaire is the progenitor of ideological irony, Henry Fielding is perhaps a source of inspiration for Parandowski's humor. Stylistically too the similarity is striking. Fielding in *Tom Jones* is imbued with the spirit of Antiquity and his literary predilections find a resonance in Parandowski's novels. The device of ending each chapter with a *cul-de-lampe* and a projection into the next, the digression and involuntary moralization, the use of Latin, all this may be paralleled in Parandowski.

As mentioned before, the narrative varies from situation to situation; it may be a simple description or a philosophical discourse. To make it livelier and more vivid the author at times makes an abrupt change; from the sublime he switches to burlesque. Another device very closely connected with this unexpected change of style is the so-called romantic irony. The somber mood is almost always destroyed by a down-to-earth expression. To give a sample of the ever present irony: an Easter feast is prepared and the Grodzickis expect a priest who annually blesses the table. Mr. Grodzicki is happy to see him, first says Parandowski, because he really liked him, and second, because after the priest's consecration the father is admitted to the bountiful table for which he hungers. Again, Father Grozd comes home and is greeted by his sister (a woman of such ugly countenance and viciousness of character as to save her from the loss of her virginity); her pious brother cannot help thinking that when the Lord resurrects the dead he might make certain exceptions. During the classroom instruction Father Grozd impatiently waits for his classes on the Gothic period, which in his thoughts merge with the position he covets in the Gothic cathedral of Lwow.

A most striking contrast is contained in a scene in which Zapotoczny, Teofil's friend, boasts about his sexual pleasures with a maid of most horrid appearance and whom, remarks the author, the pupil idealized immensely; another when Siwak, pale with emotion, listens to Zitronenblatt explain how to get to Miodowa Street and locate a bawdy house. Teofil is unimpressed; he is completely possessed by his intellectual passion. When Teofil meets the retired teacher Kalina, their first words are about Teofil's mother. True, says the author, it was not so much the mother, but a brooch she wore which Kalina noticed, and at this moment the seriousness of the conversation is broken by the author's remark that Teofil blushes: he has discovered a white thin string hanging down from the professor's fly, for Kalina has arrived at an age when it becomes increasingly difficult to keep up his appearance. And finally, when Grodzicki decides to move to a new and better apartment, the bliss of husband and wife and their plans for the future is cut short by the father's categorical if doleful ejaculation, "Have mercy upon me, Zosia, I am sick and tired of walking to the outhouse across the whole courtyard." Parandowski's language is rich and subtle, but he is not afraid to use common words and, when necessary, does not shun a certain vulgarity. Teachers use them as well as their students: one of Teofil's teachers remarks about his pupil that "Grodzicki behaves like a whore during the Polish class."

Although *Heaven in Flames* is a psychological novel and a novel of ideas, it abounds in realistic details because it is a novel of manners as well. The writer depicts with fine precision the city, the school, the principal's office, and Grodzicki's apartment. The description of the Easter table has something of the joyful festivity of Mickiewicz's *Pan Tadeusz*. Even the father's gentle and tender appellation for the food, *et caetera comestibilia,* (and other dishes) re-echoes somehow Mickiewicz's lines:

> There were likewise different dishes for the ladies
> and for the gentlemen:
> . . .
> The gentlemen had their choice of smoked meats,
> fat half-geese, hams, and slices of tongue,
> all choice, all cured in home fashion in the
> chimney with a juniper smoke.

Here are Parandowski's lines—just as affluent as the table they describe:

The table, covered with a white tablecloth, was in itself a symbol of a spring feast. The marvellous watercress, planted in a large bottle pasted over with grey blotting paper, grew into a tousled pillar of verdure. Four flower pots containing white, red, blue, and lily-colored hyacinths blended their Easter fragrance with a sunray which found its way over the roof, poked through the upper window of Father's room and through a door, slightly ajar, arrived at the crystal decanter filled with holy water, and there broke up into a multiple rainbow. The effulgence and the scent made the table, which above all appeared to be a conglomeration of forms and colors, seem light. In reality it was exceedingly heavy and opulent. In the center, rising from paperlace doilies, shining with glazed icing, topped with multicolored wreaths of glazed fruit divided by the hyacinths, stood two cakes—one made of nuts and the other a Provence cake. On one side of the table congregated the cured meats: a ham with a rosy smile, sausages blackened by juniper smoke, smoked tenderloin; on the other stood two *babas* [a traditional Easter loaf], representatives of a dozen of their kind, which on Good Friday had already emerged from their tall clay moulds. One *baba* had an incision in it so as to attest to its magnificence with its golden honey-like contents. The light nugat bar dressed in pale yellow wafers and the dark slab of layer cake symbolized other kinds of pastry for which no space could be found.

Likewise symbolic were a bottle of wine and a decanter made of blue glass and filled with cherry liqueur. And among these dignitaries of the table edged the commoners of the feast; a sugar lamb with a silver bell on a red ribbon, a piece of horseradish pared to a little stick, several eggs dyed in colors of blue, red, and green, butter in a blue-grey stoneware container and finally, on a small separate plate, sliced eggs intended for the rendering of the Easter greetings.[5]

Parandowski's use of Latin in the novel serves an important function—to unfold his characters. When Teofil's father uses it, it is to characterize the official of the Austro-Hungarian Empire who received his education at the classical gymnasium. Father Grozd's Latin is different, revealing him as a casuist whose main passion is exegesis. One of the most striking examples of a Latin phrase revealing character is Father Skromny's *"Colligite fragmenta ne pereant"* (gather the crumbs so that they will not be wasted), after breakfast, as he saves all the crumbs to throw to the sparrows on the street.

Parandowski frequently resorts to symbolism. Not reaching for the stars, it is down-to-earth and convincing. At a time when they are full of anxiety and fear for their son, the elder Grodzickis take a walk during which they encounter the fire brigade. The galloping huge black horses, sparks flying from under their hoofs, the trumpets, the glistening helmets, the embodiment of the horsemen of the Apocalypse, frighten the mother. With all the attention to the physical details, the human being is the most important element in the novel. Parandowski is a master of a subtle lyrical digression. The description of the new apartment, the nostalgic feelings of the father and mother who are unused to their new, more comfortable bedroom, their reminiscences of the old are unforgettable. The tenor of the narrative is kept within soft, mild colors and within a minor key. Parandowski's description of a young budding love between Teofil and Alina is a masterpiece; from a delicate, deeply lyrical description he progresses towards sensuous, sensual, maddening love scenes at which even Tolstoy could marvel.

II *Critics in Flames*

Heaven in Flames was greeted with a flurry of criticism and provoked a storm of controversy. One of the earlier reviewers compared the novel to Prus's short stories and Zeromski's *Syzyfowe prace* (Sisyphean Labors); he stated that the book, written with great emotional restraint, could have been a valuable aid in education, by pointing to human tendencies when people lose faith. But the author failed in this task, says the review; he chose to be indifferent to the fate of his hero.[6] Another reviewer, apparently a Catholic, saw in the book reminiscences of the writer's own school days. Gently chiding Parandowski for his supposed anti-Catholicism, he pointed to the superb construction of the novel: "Among the fruitless escapades of our contemporary novel, Teofil's inner drama, presented in a beautiful form, becomes a veritable feast for lovers of deep reflection and magnificent construction."[7]

The Catholic press sounded the alarm: "Our youth is reading *Heaven in Flames* and is losing faith," wrote a clergyman. "Who would be held responsible for this calamity? Not only Communists and free-masons" exclaimed the priest, "but writers like Parandowski, who destroy the very foundation of the state."[8]

Andrzejewski, at that time a Catholic writer, claimed that *Heaven in Flames* was only a historical novel and although it was received with great fanfare, its contents were dangerous and damaging. In spite of its interesting theme, the novel lacked any coherent purpose; it was symptomatic that he arrived at his atheism through reading. Parandowski was an artist but his "flame" lacked heat and passion; he was too "désengagé."[9]

None of the vituperative articles of the Catholic writers like
that of Skudlik, who called Parandowski a militant atheist,[10] or
Manteufflowa, who bemoaned the fact that atheism reigned
supreme in the novel,[11] could be compared in virulence to one
lengthy review in which the "critic," A. S. Aston, not only
analyzed Parandowski's "detrimental" work but also described
the sad state of religious affairs in Poland. This extensive article,
which appeared in five successive numbers of a Catholic paper,
astounds the present-day reader with its insulting tone, its
tastelessness, its lack of any critical perception and the viciousness of its political thinking.

The "review" begins by deploring the fact that a state-
supported paper, *Gazeta Polska*, should publish an anti-national
novel.[12] "One's hand trembles as one writes about blasphemous
Parandowski whose subversive methods differ but little from
those of the ungodly Bolsheviks in Russia. His atheism is that
of a caveman and his knowledge of the Holy Scripture is want-
ing. The time of faith has not passed; many statesmen in Western
Europe derive their strength and inspiration from the Catholic
Church."[13] Parandowski on the other hand," continues Aston,
"with his vulgar materialism destroys the very foundation of
the state. There are some passages in the book which indicate
that Teofil is a communist sympathizer. We know what this
leads to: when at one of the recent trials of students and
lecturers in Wilno, a girl, who was accused of being a communist,
was asked what her denomination was, answered, (oh horror!)
'none.' "[14]

Aston not only chided Parandowski and tried to redirect him
into the road of righteousness, but by quoting the articles and
paragraphs of the penal code, he clearly indicated that the
writer could and should be prosecuted for his anti-national
propaganda.[15] Aston finished his pernicious peroration by ad-
monishing the writer: "Mr. Parandowski, what happened? Why
did you publish such rot?" And finally: "The novel is mediocre,
nay, weak, from the point of view of literary construction.
Parandowski is an agitator; his guilt is shared by those who
publish him."[16]

This article was immediately seconded by another not less
biased and vehement. Its author, hiding under the initials of
J.N., claimed that Aston wrote a magnificent study which will

be of service to those who had neither read nor had any intentions of reading this anti-Christ and anti-national novel.[17] *Heaven in Flames* compromised Parandowski as a writer and as a thinking man, he claimed, and helped the people "without dogma" to sink in the quagmire of communist propaganda.[18]

Still another journalist cited *Heaven in Flames* as an example of cultural depravity which played into Jewish hands and demanded that society had not only the right but a duty to control such intellectual activity.[19]

Disturbed by the egregious virulence of these attackers, Father Wojcik appealed to Catholic writers not only to counteract such perfidious anti-national propaganda, but also to restrain themselves from the undignified outbursts of Aston.[20]

Not all of the reviewers were as vociferous and fierce in their criticism. Later, in 1946, Parandowski wrote about Karol Hubert Rostworowski (1877-1938), who joined the dispute in defense of the novel[21] and other critics who accepted *Heaven in Flames* as a great work of art, and rightfully saw that Parandowski was not an atheist, but rather someone who raised important religious questions. One of the writers, Emil Breiter, put forth the interesting thesis that Parandowski seemed to dethrone the Christian God because his beloved gods of Olympus had been already dethroned. "Teofil is a complex entity," wrote the reviewer, "not only did he lose faith, he went one step further to seek his own God. The conflict, like those of Prometheus and St. Augustine, could therefore never be resolved. The novel," continued Breiter, "was one of the best examples of Polish prose. Its vivid narrative was similar to the running sequences of motion pictures."[22]

The reputation of *Heaven in Flames* was firmly established, and as early as 1937 Kazimierz Czachowski rightfully called it a doubly modern classic: "First in the historic-cultural sense because it ideally approaches that perfect proportion, mature restraint and an unstained purity which we are accustomed to regard as the real characteristics of a classical style; and secondly in a way as a model for a classical solution of the compositional problems of fictional realism."[23]

Since then each generation has criticized, applauded and avidly read the novel; each generation has found something new in Parandowski's most popular work, not only at home but abroad. It was translated into German, Slovak, Bulgarian, Serbo-Croatian and other languages. It can be safely said now that the novel occupies an honorable and permanent place in Polish literature. Commemorating the fiftieth anniversary of Parandowski's creative activity, Jan Kulig sums up the novel's significance to the modern Polish reader. Parandowski has not only created a magnificent picture of Lwow but also depicted with rare insight the religious crisis of Teofil. He, like his predecessor the great classical scholar Zielinski, has broken away from the dead tradition of those savants (like Rojek in the novel) who petrified Antiquity. "Their expedition to the sun and to Hellenism in the twentieth century bore a splendid fruit permitting them to cut the stultifying bonds of Polish culture with the keen edge of classical antiquity."[24]

CHAPTER 5

Three Signs of the Zodiac

FOLLOWING his trip to Buenos Aires in 1936, Parandowski was as active as ever. His name appeared often in the *Wiadomosci Literackie*, and particularly in the *Gazeta Polska*, in which, as we recall, *Heaven in Flames* had been serialized. Between 1937 and 1939 Parandowski published two collections; one for children, which again was eagerly read by adults, *Three Signs of the Zodiac*, and *Visits and Encounters*, a collection of essays which had appeared earlier in various periodicals. At the same time the writer was also active as a theater critic, nor did he slacken his work as a translator, and his position as the president of the Polish PEN Club took up a considerable amount of his time.

It was in 1939, a crucial year in modern history, that Parandowski's collection of short stories *Three Signs of the Zodiac* appeared. The collection admirably summed up the years of the writer's prolific literary activity and simultaneously served as his aesthetic and spiritual credo. Each of the twenty-four stories can be detached and read as a separate entity and yet one principal idea unifies them and makes them into one inseparable whole. In his preface the author clearly defines this unifying concept which guides the reader through the collection.

The zodiac, says the writer, is comprised of twelve constellations through which the sun travels one after another. From time immemorial humanity has followed this revolution and each nation and every people has given different names to these twelve constellations. The most important annual event to hold the attention of observers was the stellar configuration at the vernal equinox, or March 21. The sun was then always under the same sign of the Zodiac, the people of early civilizations believed, since because of their relatively short life they did not notice any changes. However, changes do take place, since the earth's axis alters its direction and our planet takes a different position in reference to the stars of the zodiac and consequently there comes a time when the sun announces the spring under a different sign.[1]

Since men have begun to appear on this planet our sun has made several complete circles around the zodiac; previously human observation was too primitive to have noticed this. As the writer points out, a history of even the oldest peoples began not earlier than 5000 B.C. At that time the sun introduced spring under the sign of Taurus (the Bull), twenty centuries later it arrived under the sign of Aries (the Ram), when Christ was born it was the epoch of Pisces (the Fishes). The reader should be reminded, continues the author, that the fish had an important place among the symbols of early Christianity.[2]

The stories presented in the collection embraced the times of the Ram and Fishes; the third sign given in the title of the book is that of Aquarius which heralded our twentieth century. Mistakenly, people believed that the stars govern the fate of man, but because of their error they created mythology and poetry, thus taking cognizance and coming closer to the understanding of our planet which is but a tiny dust particle of the infinite universe. Presenting the three symbolic signs, the author strove to create a bond between our century and the forty centuries before us in which people were born and faded under the immortal stars.[3] The writer touched, in other words, upon what seemed to him the most salient, most important and the most representative moments in the history of mankind; the collection therefore is an historical excursion. Culturally too, the author tried to create a synthesis pointing to our common heritage. The religious evolution of the writer should also be noted, but this will be indicated later after several of the stories have been discussed.

Three Signs of the Zodiac begins with a general and openly didactic story, the "Egea" (Aegean Civilization). It is concluded by an equally didactic historical excursion of two modern people —father and son—into antiquity. The last powerful story, "Papiez blogoslawi" (The Holy Father Blesses), stands somewhat apart from the rest and the concluding chapter of the cycle, thus making the Cross the culminating point of our cultural heritage and our history.

If one looks at the table of contents of the collection one can easily recognize the division and the allotment of time and place to the stories which appear in chronological order. There are, aside from the three zodiacal periods, several epochs treated in the book. For convenience one could divide them into a) b) c) d) and e) periods, none of which has precise boundaries; the separation is cultural as well as temporal. The first story, "The Aegean Civilization," is really an introduction in which the author gives a general picture of the Cretan and Ionic cultures. He uses an ingenious device which enables him to superimpose modern times upon the ancient. The pivot of the story is a simple spade which is used in turn by a gardener, a well-digger and a grave-digger. The spade, says the author, although the reader might not think of it, is capable of resurrecting the dead. The allusion of course is to archeology. Thus a physical object makes it possible for the writer to unfold, as it were, a picture of the most ancient times.[1] Having thus established the tone of the narrative, the author presents a number of episodes from the life of ancient Greece. There are several different situations— Olympic games, political life of Athens, a Greek wedding and so on.

In "Wieniec olimpijski" (The Olympic Wreath) Parandowski returns to a subject dear and familiar to him—the Olympic Games. The story is a compact miniature of *The Olympic Discus*. Certainly by necessity it treats one episode only, but even so on a few pages the writer manages to recreate all the excitement and the spirit of his longer book. Consonant with the brevity and conciseness of the story is the simplicity of the Games themselves. They were much earlier than the one described in *The Olympic Discus*, and all the events and entries were simpler, as were the ceremonies.

The next story takes the reader into the political life of Athens. "The Prayer of Aristides" is a magnificent sketch of the great patriot—wronged and banished, he defends the laws of his homeland in response to the bitter indignation of his friends. Parandowski probably, among other sources, utilized the information on Aristides from Plutarch[5] who records the following incident in his *Lives:*

. . . It is reported that an illiterate, clownish fellow, giving Aristides his shard, supposing him a common citizen, begged him to write "Aristides" upon it; and he being surprised and asking if Aristides had ever done him any injury, "none at all" said he, "neither know I the man; but I am tired of hearing him everywhere called the Just." Aristides, hearing this, is said to have made no reply, but returned the shard with his own name inscribed. At his departure from the city, lifting up his hands to heaven, he made a prayer (the reverse, it would seem, of that of Achilles)[6] that the Athenians might never have any occasion which should constrain them to remember Aristides.[7]

The following story, "Ptolemy," is placed in Egypt in the third century before Christ. The decline of its former grandeur is shown in the vain frivolity surrounding the king, which the author contrasts with a picture of the old scholar Eratosthenes at solitary work in the library creating something of value for posterity.

With the next cycle, the reader moves to Rome where he encounters Cicero with his adversary, Publius Claudius, and, in the "Cherry Tree" the great orator invites himself to dinner in the house of Lucullus. It is of course a splendid feast but, as in the previous story, the guests muse about the vanity of life and fame. "Cicero will be remembered," says Lucullus, "only as long as there are people who understand Latin," but a young cherry tree picked up by Lucullus at the village of Cerasus will do for posterity much more than any man could dream of doing.

The story "In a Quarry" hints at the dawn of Christianity, and in the "Hour of History," depicting the great inundation of Rome followed by pestilence in 589, Parandowski describes Christianity firmly established, and the city, just as in "Dante," becomes a place of pilgrimage.

We then witness another great historical event, the fall of Constantinople in 1453, with the sultan, Muhammed the Second, entering the Hagia Sofia. We now move from Constantinople to Poland; the distance between them may seem great, but not to Parandowski who once wrote "Poland lies on the Mediterranean sea," stressing thereby the close affinity of Polish culture with the rest of Europe. The story, "Little Copernicus" is an evocation of the childhood of the great Polish astronomer whose discoveries so greatly changed European thinking. The name of Copernicus is to appear again in "Telescope of Galileo." The geographical setting of this extremely important story is Florence during the period of the Renaissance. "At the Court of Sigismund Augustus" introduces the old Polish capital Cracow with various representatives of the Golden Period of Polish literature. We then move into a glorious period of English literature with "The End of the Globe Theater" in which we view Elizabethan London and witness the fire which burned Shakespeare's theater in 1613. "Poczajow," a charming story with the undertones of Polish history and folklore, depicts the siege of the town by the Turks and its miraculous delivery.

As the wheels of history squeak on the reader arrives at the eighteenth century with the "Encyclopedists," a story of the ideological precursors of the French Revolution. The rest of the stories have a pronounced Polish character. "Alliance with the Sea" recounts one of the early sailing adventures of the young Joseph Conrad, later destined to attain great stature as an English novelist. It is a curious anomaly that Conrad, Polish by birth and education, never wrote a single line of fiction in his native tongue. Utilizing the cinematic device of the flash-back, Parandowski, through his hero (whose real given name was Teodor Jozef Konrad) gives us glimpses into Conrad's boyhood and family. We know his father, Apollo Nalecz Korzeniowski, as a translator of Victor Hugo and Alfred de Vigny, and as the author of a study on Shakespeare. A great patriot, he was one of the organizers of the Polish liberation movement. Then in 1861 he and his family were exiled to Vologda in northern Russia. It was on their return to Austrian Poland that his son decided to become a mariner. This story, deeply lyrical and nostalgic, reminds the reader of Antoine de Saint-Exupéry's epistle of a refugee from Estoril, Portugal. Saint-Exupéry incidently has often been compared to Conrad; what the first found in the air, under the stars, the latter found in the sea. One of the concluding stories, "Ossolineum"[8] is frankly biographical. The author goes back to his youth and to his first visit at the celebrated depository of Polish culture: the library in his native Lwow.

The Three Signs of the Zodiac covers a span of some 4,000 years, and the writer shows a certain continuity of history. Each piece in the collection is an historical short story with philosophical overtones, giving it a universal general character. What then are the most important traits of this collection? First of all

Parandowski's cultural predilection, his love for antiquity, his firm belief that our common heritage is coterminous. In this work the writer solves one of the most difficult literary problems; on a basis of realistic detail he recreates the spiritual life of various periods. Each story and each period are pregnant with ideas, nevertheless the material element of each serves as an appropriate vehicle.

Most of the stories begin with a concrete material description or an event. In the "Prayer of Aristides" the square in Athens is presented at the outset as the slaves sweep it in preparation for a shard trial. In the "House on the Palatine" the Via Appia is introduced, and Cicero returns from his banishment. One of the most striking characteristics in the collection is the device to open the story with the introduction of the principal hero; eight of the stories begin with their names. To cite only a few examples: "The young Koroibos stood in the open door . . ." ("Olympic Wreath"), "Philocrates carefully watered the last rosebush . . ." ("The Greek Wedding"), "Ptolemy, the third Egyptian king of the same name . . ." ("A Day of the King").

As soon as the principal hero is introduced, Parandowski carefully, although economically, presents his material surroundings. This is particularly evident in "The Greek Wedding" or in the "Cherry Tree"; the description of the affluent house of Lucullus and of the opulent table is significant, yet the description always serves as a bridge to the spiritual element. Some of the stories have a purely historical digression. In the "History of Constantinople," when the Venetian ship moves out of the harbor, people on board begin to reminisce, a device enabling the author to give a cursory history of Byzantium. The reader is reminded that many years ago, around 660 B.C. another ship headed by Byzas was moving to the place where the great city was founded. In 324 Constantine proclaimed the city the capital of the eastern section of the Empire, and after the fall of Rome it became the capital of the world. In the sixth century A.D. while Western Europe was ossifying in the state of barbarity, Byzantine civilization, under the long and wise reign of Justinian and his heirs, flourished—its cultural influence overflowing its geographical boundaries and playing a decisive role in the cultural formation of the people living on a vast territory stretching from Bulgaria to Persia and in the north, from Kiev to Novgorod.

Sometimes an historical event does not necessitate this kind of historical discourse. For instance, the "End of the Globe Theater" begins with a specific date; and the author does not have to digress to provide historical background. Nor does he go beyond the fire of the theater. Reminiscences are important in "Ossolineum," and again the writer is concrete and comes right to the point: "I shall never forget the day when for the first time I was going to the Ossolineum." From the description of this particular day, from personal experience, Parandowski progresses to the general picture of the Ossolineum and its importance in preserving the monuments of Polish culture.

The dialogue, as in many instances before, is important in Parandowski's collection. In one of the stories, "At the Court of Sigismund Augustus," with Polish history as a background, it is of paramount importance. The story begins in the morning and ends late at night. Father Kochanowski wakes up his brother, the celebrated Jan Kochanowski (1530-1584), the first truly Polish poet. A contemporary and a reputed acquaintance of Ronsard, he wrote in vernacular at the same time giving Polish poetry broader connection with European literature and enabling it to become more universal. Only one day in the life of the great man is depicted, but how significant and how representative this day is. Kochanowski walks through the courtyard of Wawel castle encountering to his utmost chagrin a somewhat boorish country squire, Koscien, who desires to be introduced to the King. After a conversation in the castle and an unsuccessful attempt to rid himself of his bothersome companion, Kochanowski meets his friend Gornicki (another historical personage), the King's secretary. Meanwhile, Koscien (who is not unlike Sienkiewicz's character, Zagloba, or Shakespeare's Falstaff) crashes through to the King's study, giving Parandowski an opportunity to describe both the King and the historical environment of Wawel.

The company then moves to the tavern to drink Cracow beer and to have a lusty conversation which turns into an argument about famous Mikolaj Rej, the writer of frivolous and at times coarse and prurient facetiae. Koscien, claiming to be a friend of Rej, defends his Polish writings against Kochanowski and the Polish "Paduans" in the group. Late at night, Kochanowski returns to his quarters in the castle. Suffering from insomnia he composes his verse "To Sleep."

This then is the day of Polish history. How much Parandowski was able to depict in such a short story! Aside from recreating the historical, physical setting, presenting a portrait of a somewhat light-hearted King, he touches upon the cultural as well as everyday life of old Cracow with its society and literary conflicts. The story, kept within subdued honey-like colors, mellow and Renaissance like Wawel itself with a sprinkle of the golden brilliance of Boticelli, is exceedingly realistic as well as gently humorous. Koscien, lacking the strictness of the Chamberlain in *Pan Tadeusz,* defends national Polish customs and at times serves as a comic relief. Parandowski achieves this by a juxtaposition of this Polish squire and his down-to-earth habits of speech with the refined and sophisticated gentlemen educated abroad. These contrasting styles are also used by the author with comical effect. At times one sentence punctures the elated mood in the story. One of the gentlemen plays the lute, singing an idyl, he is congratulated by the company who compares him to Theocritus. The writer destroys this particular mood by an interjection: "Koscien, leaning on a wall, was snoring." It is Kochanowski, deeply rooted in Latin culture, who serves as a link between the new and the old tradition, which as the reader will recall, is an historical truism.

Another instance from the history of the Polish-Lithuanian commonwealth finds its expression in "Poczajow," a charming little town with the Basilian monastery located in the province of Volhynia. The times depicted are anything but charming; this is the period of Turkish invasion. The story again is an example of how Parandowski utilizing a realistic setting discloses a fantastic, almost grotesque situation. It also lays bare the author's literary device of "making strange." The people presented in this tale naïvely accept the miracles and strange events, and the reader is compelled to do likewise.

The writer begins his narrative with: "On a bald mountain above Horyn stood devil Harab dressed like a gamekeeper." Harab is visited by another devil, Farel, who is innocuous but not by choice, and a conversation ensues between the two. Harab complains that he received an order from the Grand Master—Lucifer himself—to lead the plundering Turks to Poczajow: "It is about time," remarked the master, "to finish off those monks." To Farel's jubilant exclamation Harab retorts that having lived for ages in this countryside and having played all kinds of tricks and mischief on its inhabitants, he has grown "devilishly" fond of Poczajow. Having accomplished his sinister duty with a heavy heart the sentimental devil leaves the stage.

Meanwhile there is a great commotion in town. It is rumored that two events taking place are portents of evil. The holy icon begins to shed tears, and simultaneously some peasants report to have seen Hadyna, a very ugly and odious monster, portending draught, pestilence or some other disaster. The Turkish advance troops reach Poczajow, and the populace rallies to its defense, repelling a supine attempt of the enemy to breach the walls. Suddenly and inexplicably the horde beats a hasty retreat. The peasants arriving in the town the next morning explain the miracle: in the heavens they saw the Virgin Mary with a hundred or perhaps a thousand, or perhaps ten thousands angels (who would think of counting them?) in shining armor and with their swords ablaze. In great panic and confusion the disorganized Turks run away. The zealous Harab tries to stop them, makes roaring noises, leads them into a swamp, but his efforts to turn the infidels back to Poczajow come to naught. The story ends with the thanksgiving service and a *lírnik,* a blind itinerant singer composing a Ukrainian song about the deliverance of Poczajow.

The author took an historical event of 1675 and made it into a realistic story, realistic in the same way as Gogol's novelettes and "Old Russian Military Tales." Parandowski renders the supernatural element more credible by humanizing his devils to some degree. Their speech is only slightly different from that of the rustics. Their clothing is like that of humans, a device also used by Marlow in dressing his devil like a gentleman. Similarly, the Mephistopheles of Goethe, attired in the same inconspicuous way, berates the witch who asks why he has no hooves, tail or claws, explaining: "Ich bin ein Kavalier wie andre Kavaliere."[9]

The most striking example of Parandowski's method of progressing from the physical environment is contained in the story called "The Encyclopedists." The author begins by what can be called a reversed fenestration device; he opens the story by literally looking through the window of Diderot's house:

"Straight from the street, one can see the entire room." In a first short paragraph the author turns the attention of the reader to the contents of the room, thus making it known what the inhabitant's inclinations are. On the bookshelves there are Homer, Vergil, Horace, Cicero—the owner of the room is clearly steeped in classical culture. The reader is not yet told whose room it is; it could have belonged to any one of the encyclopedists. The furniture and the material setting attest to the man's profession. He obviously is a writer. Having presented the material setting Parandowski concludes this remarkably full paragraph by a simple sentence—"Here lives Diderot."

Then Parandowski confesses that all this was nothing but a device, there is no such room or house in existence. However, muses the writer, it did exist at one time. The author then presents another association: "Deep inside the room there was a door," says Parandowski, and here he adds the words of the philosopher himself: "Everytime I hear knocking at my door I am afraid to open it." What a rich sentence, so significant in consequence! Quite logically, Parandowski interjects: "He was afraid to open the door in that eighteenth century in which he lived." In three short paragraphs the writer, beginning with a concrete physical background, presents the man who is primarily known for his spirit and intellect. After the exposition and introduction there is but one step to a description of the compilation of the famous Encyclopedia finished in 1772 with its contributors Jean-Jacques Rousseau, Holbach, Helvetius and even Voltaire. The concluding vignette to this instructive story is the significance of the Encyclopedists' efforts and activities and their ideological role in the French Revolution.

Nature plays a secondary, supporting role in Parandowski's collection. Sometimes, however, it acquires a greater meaning, serving as an introduction to the tenor of the narrative; it becomes its key. "Alliance with the Sea" has a reconciliatory character bordering on resignation. It is permeated with a natural element, the role of which is no longer subordinate.

A better example of the role of nature setting the tone of the narrative, at the same time expressing the spirit of reconciliation, and one dares to say amalgamation of ideas, is contained in "The Telescope of Galileo": "From the nearby banks of the Arno the fragrance of the myrtle moved through the calm air." This first phrase reveals the mood of the story. On the upper terrace of Palazzo Vecchio preparations are being made for a great feast; the Grand Duke of Florence, Cosimo dei Medici, accompanied by his wife and his guests (among whom is Galileo, another celebrated son of Florence), arrive for the festive and sumptuous dinner. The great astronomer tells the guests, including several dignitaries of the Church, about his telescope and his discoveries which support the theories of Copernicus. In great disbelief and bewilderment the Duke and some of the guests look through the telescope. Padre Ceccini attacks Galileo's teaching as contrary and noxious to the Church's doctrine and proclaims it a heresy. Galileo asks for indulgence, and declares that he is a faithful servant of the Church, and his ideas only support the infinite wisdom of God. At this point Prior Maraffi embraces Galileo and exclaims: "Brother, you speak like a true Christian." The Duke, greatly embarrassed and confused at first, leads Galileo to the table and places him next to his seat.

The message of this sophisticated and refined tale, the dramatis personae of which carry on such a brilliant and mellifluous conversation, is clear. Parandowski, prudently omitting the trial of Galileo by the Holy Inquisition and the abjuration of his teachings (under the threat of torture) which were found inimical to the Church's doctrine, brings peace and reconciliation between two incompatible parties. Parandowski condenses the events in his historical sketch, creating an epitome, and deflects his narrative from the historical truth.

A curious incident and a classical example of literary parallelism occurred at this time. In 1938-39 another writer created a play about Galileo. It is highly unlikely that the two men knew anything about each other's work. The play, Bertolt Brecht's *Leben des Galileo*, was staged for the first time in Switzerland in 1943, when Parandowski was fighting for his bare existence. Its scope is greater than Parandowski's story; it is tendentious and its thesis is applicable to our modern age. What is so remarkable about the two stories is that their historical and literary components are very much alike, not in the sense that both writers utilize the same historical source material, but that each uses the same expressions, although giving them absolutely different meanings. One of the most striking examples is the offer of Galileo to look through the telescope. In Parandowski's story,

at the first hint of a conflict, Galileo asks for indulgence and
receives it. Brecht's Galileo desperately begs people to look
through the telescope so that they might see with their own
eyes, but everyone scornfully turns away. "Recantation was a
crime," writes Brecht in his notes, "and an 'original sin' which
was a serious setback for science." Posterity was too kind to
Galileo, creating a legend about his last statement after the
trial; Brecht analyzes Galileo's act from a moral as well as a
sociological point of view:

I hope this work shows what society extorts from its individuals, what
it needs from them. The urge to research, a social phenomenon no
less delightful or compulsive than the urge to reproduce, steers
Galileo into that most dangerous territory, drives him into agonizing
conflict with his violent desires for other pleasures. He raises his
telescope to the stars and delivers himself to the rack. In the end
he indulges his science like a vice, secretly and probably with pangs
of conscience. Confronted with such a situation, one can scarcely
wish only to praise or only to condemn Galileo.[10]

Parandowski, on the other hand, looks at the tragic incident
(Brecht refused to call his play a tragedy) from the modern,
secular point of view. That is, he looks at it through the eyes
of the present-day Church which found its way to tolerance
through a morass of crimes and persecutions. This is an important
story from the ideological point of view; for it marks a turning
point in the writer's ideological make-up and is perhaps a
spiritual addendum to his *Heaven in Flames*.

The last story in Parandowski's collection would seem to
support this thesis. The writer consolidates his position, so to
say, by moving to modern times and depicting an audience
with the Pope. The story has all the splendor and pageantry of
the Vatican and the magnificence of Saint Peter's square. But
with all the glorification of the Church and the description of
the elation of the people at the sight of the Holy Father,
Parandowski introduces a Trojan Horse into his story. The comparison of the Vatican with the headquarters of an army and
the huge registration file and keeper of souls is convincing, as
is the almost mass psychosis of the crowd. But the description
of the organization which Brecht called the "Authority" embodied

in one man is frightening. Parandowski shows a great acuity and historical sense in concluding his collection with his description of the cosmopolitan Vatican, symbol of universality. *Three Signs of the Zodiac* proves Parandowski to be a writer of a special, erudite philosophical and historical story. This genre will predominate in his later work. Ideologically he moves slightly away from paganism and devotes more attention to Roman Catholicism; this trend will become more evident and pronounced in his later years. It should be borne in mind, however, that he is too deeply rooted in ancient culture to become a religious writer.[11] As in previous books, he stresses the essential, the permanent and what seems to him universal and lasting in our civilization.

In literary life Parandowski refuses to join any group and preserves his Olympian calm and independence. The name Olympian is more and more often applied to him, which the author resents, notwithstanding its flattering implication. He claims that the name spells detachment, which is different from independence. His Olympian calm is also deceptive, implying that no matter what happens around him he is undaunted, which was never true. Hence his many unfulfilled projects and ideas. The writer has to have absolute peace around him in order to be productive. His impeccable style, too, is a result of self-discipline and is attained by hard labor and concerted effort.

＊　＊　＊　＊　＊

The year 1939 finds Parandowski in the prime of his life. His reputation as a writer and translator is firmly established and unchallenged. He is full of energy and plans for the future. He had recently conceived the idea of writing a second part to *Heaven in Flames* in which Teofil was to be depicted as a mature person and as a man of action. The times were foreboding in 1938 — Austria fell victim to German expansion and was incorporated in the Third Reich. As the president of the Polish PEN center Parandowski was able to render assistance to various fugitive writers. One of the refugees, Franz Theodor Csokor, presently chairman of the Austrian PEN, remembers with great warmth all the kind help Parandowski accorded him, including the acquisition of a Polish passport which made his life more tolerable.

In the summer of 1939, on his way from Palestine to Sweden, the Hebrew writer Saul Czernichowski (1875-1943) tried to persuade the Parandowskis also to retire to Sweden. The family debated and wavered and decided not to go. Later the writer did not regret his decision to stay behind—"No matter how monstrously difficult a time it was, I am happy that I remained with my people, suffering through all the privations and moral degradations." Unaware how soon Poland was to walk the road to Calvary the family moved to Swider. Poland, called once by one of her greatest sons "the Christ of nations," was about to embark on yet another road of Passion.

CHAPTER 6

September Night *and the War*

Nessun maggior dolore
che ricordarsi del tempo felice
nella miseria.

—Dante

Il n'est pas de commune mesure entre
le combat libre et l'écrasement dans
la nuit. Il n'est pas de commune
mesure entre le métier de soldat et
le métier d'otage. Vous êtes les
saints.

—Antoine de Saint-Exupéry

ON September 1, 1939, Germany opened hostilities against the Polish state. On a broad front, the German army hurled its might against Poland from the west and in the south. Eight days later, an advance division stood close to Warsaw. The Polish government and the High Command had already fled the capital for Lublin.

Soon, practically all organized resistance ceased. By the middle of the month the Germans were everywhere in western Poland, and on September 17, the Soviet Union, in fulfillment of the Hitler-Stalin pact, invaded and occupied eastern Poland.

The first of September found Parandowski and his family in Swider at Villa Sloneczna. Just the day before the Tuwims had arrived, and the two men sat glued to their radio sets listening to the disquieting war news. Even after the outbreak of hostilities very few people could fathom the catastrophe. Events moved with cataclysmic rapidity. A few days later friends and families separated, finding their way into exile or roaming around Poland. Tuwim left the country, eventually spending his war years in the United States.

Parandowski remained in Poland. On September 5, he and his family arrived in Warsaw, finding the city in uproar and chaos. The next day they set out for Lwow, another voyage which the writer later called the last voyage of the Odyssey. September 7 was spent in an overcrowded train, which somehow did not move along. Not far from Krzywda the train was bombed and strafed, and the family found it advisable to rely on their own means of transportation, walking on the eighth and the ninth to Gutow and Adamow in the direction of Kock. Their experiences during the days which followed are set down in a memoir, entitled *September Night,* a vivid collection of essays published in 1962.

Fall is a beautiful season in most countries and this September was an exceptionally fine one. On the road the Parandowskis met many refugees, who, like them, walked looking to the sky for rain which could make the roads impassable for German motorized troops and cover the sky from ever-present German planes which dominated the roads and shot at anything.

Many Europeans remember those all too familiar flights—the overcrowded huts, the lack of food—although there was always someone who would sell it or give it away. If a hut was particularly crowded there was nothing wrong with spending the night in a haystack. September nights are beautiful in Poland.

Until the end of September Parandowski and his family remained at the settlement of Jaloszynska. Here they witnessed the last engagement of that campaign—the Battle of Kock—and saw German soldiers for the first time. In his *September Night,* Parandowski described this first encounter. Germans run into the village firing sub-machine guns; worried about her children, Parandowski's wife calmly steps out and tells the soldiers that there is no sense shooting up a peaceful village. So great is the surprise of the enemy that the shooting stops. Many years later Madame Parandowski described this incident to the present writer. Endowed with a great dramatic talent she made her description vivid and realistic, and one could easily see how German soldiers were baffled by her effervescent personality.

The journey was not over yet. The family moved to Czemerniki where it saw the last Polish soldiers trying to escape German prisoner of war camps. And then to Lubartow, spending a week there.[1] October suddenly brought rain, wind, sleet and snow.

Cold and miserable, the family set out for Lublin on the thirteenth in a quaint diligence drawn by a pair of old horses. A
day or two later Parandowski was walking on Krakowskie Przed-
miescie[2] taking painful cognizance of the physical presence of
the Germans in the country. The street was plastered over with
their posters of official announcements—proclamations placing
the nation in bondage.

In Lublin Parandowski and his family found refuge at the
Catholic University in the apartment of Professor Jakubanis who
was absent. The University was ready to begin another term
when the Germans occupied it and removed everybody from its
premises. Although the family was able to find some private quarters in the city, their physical privations were great; Parandowski
was spending his last *zloty* and was looking for some sort of
work. A principal of a girls' secondary school offered him a
position as teacher of logic in the school.

Parandowski prepared his first lecture with great care and
enthusiasm. "Happiness," its topic, was possibly suggested by
his reading at this time of Diogenes' *Laertios*. Or perhaps grief
and calamity were his inspiration, since the thought of happiness is most persistent at a time of defeat and disaster. It was
not accidental, Parandowski remarked, that Professor Tatarkie-
wicz wrote a beautiful book entitled *On Happiness* during the
horrors of the German occupation. As Parandowski delivered this
initial lecture he was acutely aware of the great attention his
young students gave to his words.[3] He began with the etymology
of the word "Philosophy," discussing its earliest history until he
arrived at the period when Aristotle, Socrates and Plato created
the new discipline of logic.

But this was the only opportunity Parandowski had to talk to
the children. When he came back to school two days later he
heard the bad news: the Germans had ordered the school building vacated. Several times the writer returned to the school
building around which some teachers and pupils clustered to
exchange war news and rumors. The situation was hopeless
even for the most convinced optimists. Parandowski's family
continued to suffer privations and now had to find other shelter
for the coming winter. Luckily he was invited to Strzyzewice,
some twenty kilometers from Lublin.[4] The family moved around
Christmas time, living through one of the coldest Polish winters.[5]

In the spring of 1940 Parandowski and his family decided to go back to Warsaw. To their great and pleasant surprise the apartment on Filtrowa Street was untouched, although some strangers were living in it.[6] Parandowski does not like to dwell on the wartime conditions in Warsaw, but *Wrzesniowa noc* (September Night) is one of the few works which touches on it. He is frugal in his description not because he was passive, but perhaps because he thinks these things are better forgotten. In one of the numerous conversations between myself and Zbigniew Parandowski, the writer's son, I pointed to Jan Parandowski's little granddaughter and wondered aloud whether she would ever learn of the cruel events which had happened in Warsaw, now reborn like a phoenix from the ashes. Her father was vehement. "What purpose would it serve," he said, "to poison a child's mind with memories of events so horrible and of such monstrous scope that even a normal grown-up human being would not comprehend them?"

Perhaps another reason for Parandowski's silence is that he feels the horrors of the war are beyond the imagination of those who were not there. Writing about the first postwar congress of the PEN Club held in Stockholm, he said that participants from the neutral countries or countries little affected by the war listened to him in disbelief.

In *September Night,* however, Parandowski described how the family spent one day in Warsaw. It was more than an ordinary day. The family seldom ventured outside their apartment block, but on this day the elder Parandowskis set out to deliver a completed chapter of a book to the publisher. The arrangement with the publisher was that the work would be published after the war. Parandowski would receive a small advance, a pittance of 300 zlotys for his chapter. It was a "tradition" then that the husband and wife would stop on the way home and buy some pastry. First carefully selected, it was then equally carefully divided in the family. The children would be happy then, but the family's joy was a very brief respite for them in an otherwise barren existence.

By presenting this one day in the life of his family, Parandowski created a picture suggestive of everyday life. Iwaszkiewicz claimed that the author of this otherwise magnificent collection was too self-centered[7] but it is precisely because it is a collection of personal observant and brilliant memoir-like sketches that the book is powerful and convincing in its veracity. The period between the family's departure from Warsaw and the time when the invaders were expelled from the country is missing in the book. The family felt relatively safe in the country and the sojourn there did not really fit into that dark "September" spirit.

The Parandowskis seldom received anyone, and the mail was delivered on rare occasions. It was just as well; it was safer to be forgotten. To every German appeal or ordinance, Parandowski turned a deaf ear, be it registration for work duty or signing up for any literary activity. Even the telephone was disconnected and removed. Only once did Parandowski respond to a decree of the German administration, when in 1942 it ordered that all subjects of non-German nationality were to register and receive proper identification cards without which anyone caught in Warsaw would be regarded a rebel. Sometimes the writer would dare to go to the post-office to pick up the parcels which miraculously found their way from some neutral country. Food was scarce, but coffee, real genuine coffee, a rarity in occupied Europe, was often in plentiful supply in Parandowski's household, received as gifts from friends in more fortunate countries untouched by war.

I "Balsam for my Soul"

Parandowski's only solace was his work. "It was an ideal situation," he remarked. "Writing in those days was balsam for my soul."[8] He immersed himself in antiquity and in the Renaissance, and he began the second part of his *Heaven in Flames*. Unfortunately the manuscript perished during the Warsaw uprising and Parandowski never resumed work on it. "It would have been like writing a different book," the author stated, "other more immediate projects overshadowed the second part of the novel."

Careful readers of Parandowski may sense that a spiritual transformation took place within him during those years; a conjecture supported by a statement of the writer himself. "It was during the occupation that I regained faith and became again a convinced and practising Catholic." This statement by no means signifies that Parandowski became a pronounced Catholic writer, even if he might prefer to consider himself as such. It will be discussed at a later point to what degree his conversion affected his writings.[9] To many Polish intellectuals Catholicism is an

integral part of West European Civilization. What irony that
Poland, "the rampart of the Christian civilization," should suffer
at the hands of a nation which was supposed to be organizing
a new order in Europe. How must Parandowski, who shortly
before wrote, "Poland lies on the Mediterranean Sea," have felt
at the time of this nightmare. Perhaps it was the fight for bare
existence which saved him from a serious doubt; this is something for future historians to find out.

The harshness of war-time reality did not detract the author
from his interest and preoccupation with antiquity. Thus "On
the 21st of April 754 B.C. Rome was born," began another
ambitious project—*Rzym* (Rome)—a historio-psychological portrait. Parandowski had scrupulously made many notes during his
pre-war travels in Italy, carefully noting the landscape, geography
and historical monuments.

More than 200 pages of this manuscript were completed by
the end of the war. To this day their fate is shrouded in mystery.
The original was destroyed in the fire at the apartment house in
Filtrowa Street after the uprising, and a second copy, brought
to the Atlas Publishing House for safekeeping with a view to
its postwar publication, disappeared along with other papers
of his after the destruction of Warsaw. Although the Publishing
House was destroyed, the manuscripts in its cellar all escaped
destruction with the single exception of Parandowski's manuscript, not a single sheet of which has since been found. To the
writer himself this disappearance remains a riddle; was it
destroyed, misplaced or stolen?

Also during the war, Parandowski undertook a translation of
Caesar's *Commentarii de bello civili* of which the first and the
second parts disappeared like his other writings in the Publishing
House. The third part remained in the Ossolineum. After the
war Parandowski again translated the first two parts, and his
C. I. Caesar: O wojnie domowej was published in 1951.

In spite of the comfort Parandowski found in his writing, life
in Warsaw grew increasingly difficult and dangerous. The Polish
underground, unwilling to risk losing one of its most prominent
writers, urged him to leave the city. Thus in the summer of 1942
the family moved to Planta, a village in the country. Here food
was more readily available, and the family lived relatively unperturbed until 1944.

CHAPTER 7

Return to Work — Postwar Reappraisals

THE spring and summer of 1944 saw a change in the military situation in Europe. Soviet forces entered Polish territories, taking Lwow on July 27. A few days later, they took Planta, where the Parandowskis had remained since their flight from Warsaw.

The war was not over, however. The Germans counter-attacked and the farm on which the Parandowskis were hiding became a no-man's land. The family spent several days in an underground storehouse in the middle of a vegetable garden. The artillery fire was so intense from both sides that hundreds of shells exploded in the garden. Their situation was made even more unbearable by the fact that Madame Parandowski expected a child any day. So it was decided to move back to the Russian side and find a safer spot. After a long and dangerous trip, the family arrived in Tarnobrzeg where on September 23, under most difficult conditions, Madame Parandowski gave birth to another son, Piotr. The family then found refuge in the palace of Count Tarnowski in nearby Dzikow, later to be moved again to an estate near Lublin.

The war was coming to an end. On January 17, 1945, Warsaw was liberated from the Germans but lay in ruins; the people at once began to return to their homes and clear the passages between the obliterated buildings. "Not for one second," wrote Parandowski "did I have the slightest doubt that our capital would be rebuilt."

Zbigniew Parandowski, the writer's eldest son, set out on a reconnaissance mission and reported that the apartment house on Filtrowa Street was burned out. After the insurgents had surrendered, the German army, following orders to eradicate the city, moved in with flamethrowers and put the remaining intact houses to the torch. When Zbigniew came to the burnt-out shell of their building and entered the familiar apartment he was horrified to see his father's library. The books were burnt but still stood like empty tombs on the shelves; when he touched them they crumbled into ashes. The loss of his library deeply wounded Parandowski; he refers to it frequently afterwards both in his writings and in conversation.

Fortunately for the family Parandowski was now invited by the Senate of the reopened Lublin Catholic University to accept an appointment as Dean and to organize the department of comparative literature, a position in which he proved not only an able and erudite professor, but a good administrator as well. Thus began one of the joyous periods in the writer's life. He had a sense of accomplishment and his wife was not idle either— she organized, managed and ably directed a theater for children "Nasz Teatr" (Our Theater). All the participants worked with great enthusiasm, staging improvised plays from Homer and Polish classics, beginning with Kochanowski and ending with Mickiewicz and other Polish romanticists.

When Warsaw was partially rebuilt the family moved to the capital, with Parandowski driving down to Lublin to deliver his lectures and to discharge his duties as dean. But the inconvenience of travel, further preoccupation with his writings and his somewhat failing health forced him to give up his professorship in 1950; henceforth all of his time was devoted to writing. His wife likewise gave up her position as a director of the theater in order to devote all of her energies to her husband, who was somewhat chagrined at this self-sacrifice and devotion.

The first few postwar years Parandowski spent contributing to the general cultural rebuilding of the country, lecturing in various proliferating institutions; the stupendous tasks the Polish people had before them defied imagination and the obstacles at times seemed to be insurmountable, but such was the will of this tenacious nation that the physical and spiritual wounds began to heal. After the years of literary inactivity and intellectual vacuum the literate public now voraciously craved good books which they read with almost insatiable appetite. His entire wartime work gone, Parandowski re-edited and republished his early works; *Three Signs of the Zodiac*, second edition 1945, *Heaven in Flames*, 1946, *Olympic Discus*, two editions, 1946 and 1948, and *The Two Springs*.

Poland again reappeared on the map of Europe, but its peace was marred by internal as well as external problems, aggravated by the fact that there were two rival governments vying for power, one in London established shortly after the collapse of the state in September, 1939, and another, the Lublin Committee, backed by the Soviet Union and formed in 1944. The latter ultimately triumphed.

With the re-establishment of the Polish state many writers had to make a choice—some returned to Poland from the Soviet Union or from the West; others remained abroad. Some intellectuals who remained in Poland during the war got out at the first opportunity. Parandowski remained somewhat aloof from political controversy, preparing to devote himself to the rehabilitation of the country. His humanistic philosophy, which permitted him to consider only the lasting, the permanent in life, saved him from any transient controversy. Temporary political storms and their consequences affected him but little.

Among other organizations in postwar Poland was the rejuvenated PEN Club. In 1946 Parandowski received a questionnaire in which he was asked what in his opinion should be the site of the next congress of the International Federation. The writer was not unique in his answer; most of the European members craved to meet in the calm, hospitable surroundings of Stockholm which had been the proposed meeting place for 1939, cut short by the war. In 1946 Parandowski and his entire family received an invitation to the World PEN Club meeting, applied for and received a passport, and departed for the unravished shores of Sweden. At last the Parandowskis had refuge from all the memories of war days and could relax in an atmosphere of social stability and enjoy food which was denied most Europeans, including the victorious British.

One day at a formal reception Parandowski was introduced to a compatriot, a lecturer at Stockholm University, who had come to Sweden shortly before the war to work towards his doctorate at Uppsala University. The two families soon became friendly and spent many an hour together reminiscing and discussing various literary and scholarly projects. Zbigniew Folejewski, now a professor at one of the Canadian universities, recalls that it was in Stockholm that Parandowski began to write his *Powrot do zycia* (Return to Life) and spoke about a col-

lection of essays entitled *Alchemia słowa* (The Alchemy of the
Word). Questioned about his plans and intentions and whether
he would like to stay abroad, the writer replied categorically
in the negative: "I want to go back to Poland and do not con-
template any life outside her boundaries."[1]

After the meeting in Stockholm, the Parandowskis went to
Norway as guests of the Norwegian PEN Club—a pleasant and
profitable trip—and then made a detour to France for a short
time on their way home. To Parandowski, as to many Poles,
France is the center of European civilization. Thus it was with
intense interest that the writer visited libraries, museums,
churches and the Sorbonne. Moving about Paris he observed
closely the everyday life of the people, which, as in any of the
recently liberated countries, was difficult. Yet as he watched the
warm, human vitality in the streets and savored the gentle
luminosity of the skies of the Ile-de-France it seemed to Parandowski that fabled Paris was already beginning to glow again
with the incandescence she had radiated over Europe during
long centuries. French intellectuals, like the general population,
were still smarting from the effects of the occupation. To many
it had been a struggle against the German occupation; for some,
death in the concentration camps; and for others collaboration
with the enemy. The general level of contemporary literature did
not seem to him as rich as it had been after the First World War.
Only one writer, Sartre, became extremely popular, initiating a
new literary movement, existentialism. Although he thought that
the author of *Mort sans sépulture,* and *La Putain respectueuse*
was undoubtedly endowed with originality and talent, Parandowski was rather cool to Sartre's works,[2] claiming that he
would lie if he were to say that the reading of *Le Mur* gave
him any aesthetic enjoyment.

"The images, which fill the book, are for the most part disgusting,
worse than the images with which Céline fed his cynics, and no revela-
tion of the world result from it. Once again we see how difficult it is
to present a man through sexual organs, his "innards" and "excrements."[3]

Parandowski, a keen drama critic in the 1930's, followed
theater life in Paris with interest and enthusiasm, noting with
satisfaction that the repertory always included the French classics

and that the box offices did a thriving business. A few days before his departure he was invited to the modest house of André Gide for a pleasant conversation, about the outcome of the war and the fate of Poland. Gide offered Parandowski some tickets to attend *Hamlet,* performed in Gide's translation. On the last day the writer bade goodbye to Notre-Dame de Paris perceiving in it a symbol of unity and human dignity embodied in the Catholic Church.

After almost a year's absence and to the great surprise of many, the family returned to participate in the rebuilding of the cultural heritage of their country. To Parandowski it meant a number of new works, sometimes bitter disappointments, but also his finest hours of triumph.

I *Postwar Reappraisals*

The first postwar years in Poland are marked by search and experimentation in literature, both in method and ideology. One Polish writer described the mood:

The Yalta agreement between the Western allies and the Soviet Union had the unexpected result of transforming Poland into a laboratory resort where the most incompatible elements of human destiny are melting into new forms of co-existence. The living cells in that uncanny crucible—brains, hearts, red and white blood corpuscles—still simmer, producing reactions and mixtures, sputtering anger, exuding hope, in preparation for synthesis to come. This in Poland is not a time for achievement; it is a time for building and experimenting.[4]

But the building and experimenting produced achievement. Inspired by the recent horrors of the war, by opposing ideologies, by the social and political ferment of postwar Europe, by the struggle for literary freedom, and by the labors of their nation to be reborn intellectually and rebuilt physically, Polish writers and artists in all fields hastened to work. In literature and art, in theater and in the motion picture industry, Poles experimented boisterously and vigorously. Parandowski's genius blossomed with renewed energy; he began with a reappraisal and re-evaluation of his former work.

The third, but first postwar, edition of *Heaven in Flames,* attracted attention from the critics in 1947: a number of short reviews of an informative character were generally positive in their appraisal. One reviewer called its republication a valuable contribution to Polish belles lettres.[5] Another noted that the writer claimed to have changed his views after the war, yet the novel, the hero of which is so intransigent that nothing can sway him from his quest, is of such high universal level that Parandowski's spiritual transformation in no way makes him inconsistent. "The book indeed is aflame, and what should be particularly stressed is that in spite of its heavy intellectual content it never loses its epic brilliance."[6] Still another reviewer greeted the novel as an important milestone in the history of Polish prose. "The book, written in the most brilliant prose, an example of the highest artistic creation, need a reappraisal and re-evaluation since before the war it, as some readers will recall, provoked such a vivid controversy."[7]

In a lengthy article another Polish critic, Jadwiga Kulczycka-Saloni, attempted to analyze *Heaven in Flames,* pointing out the satisfaction with which it would be greeted by the readers. After a thorough investigation of the plot the critic turned her attention to certain "flaws" in it: a too minute description of Lwow, a love for microscopic detail, disturbed her. The society described by Parandowski is like Pompei—static, preserved as if covered by the lava of time.[8] This is the first note of criticism levelled at the writer for not relating the social problems of modern Poland to the earlier period depicted in the book. The *Olympic Discus,* according to the same critic, is the creation of a scholar, rather than a writer of fiction. The superabundance of *realia* might scare an ordinary average reader who would want to read for relaxation. Nevertheless, she said, the book is valuable as it has certain didactic qualities and may arouse special interest in antiquity among schoolchildren.

Very interesting was the attitude of the Catholic or Catholic-oriented critics. One reviewer, Stefan Papee, apparently a high school teacher, made an interesting experiment in his classroom; he made *Heaven in Flames* obligatory reading material. The students, disturbed at first at the "scandalous" reputation of the novel but prompted by their teacher, discovered that the book was by no means anti-Catholic.[9]

Another reviewer, oddly enough bearing the same name as the hero in *Heaven in Flames,* pointed out that the novel was misunderstood at the time of its publication in being erroneously considered an anti-Catholic work. The novel gives food for thought and points out what happens to Catholics when they are not sufficiently prepared to cope with their religious conflicts. Parandowski's work is a good school for young writers in regard to literary technique, composition and style.[10]

These two unorthodox articles mark a reconciliation of the Catholic writers with Parandowski's controversial novel. Let us note, however, that now the critics of the left expressed alarm at the change in Parandowski's world outlook. In a lengthy article, another Polish critic, Adolf Sowinski, opens a review with a discussion of the introduction to the third edition. *Heaven in Flames,* according to this critic, is characterized not only by the brilliance of the prose, but by valuable philosophical contents. Disturbed by Parandowski's pronouncements and assertations about the change in his world outlook, Sowinski expressed hope that the writer would continue the second part in the same vein as the first and would remain a sophisticated psychologist of the religious crisis, which is so characteristic of the first part of the novel—a book of a decidedly progressive nature.[11]

Still another critic, Mieczyslaw Jaroslawski, discussed Parandowski's work from the point of view of its philosophical content; the title of the article itself was indicative: "On the Periphery of Reality." In truth, its author was only on the periphery of serious criticism. The general tenor of the article was favorable to Parandowski although not devoid of a certain undercurrent of apologia. The critic found Parandowski's literary method too scholarly and exact, while his mode of reasoning betrayed an affinity with Platonic and Aristotelian dislike for the peremptory. Thanks to the further influence of Bergson and Einstein, Jaroslawski claimed, Parandowski consolidated it as a factual and correct approach to observed phenomena.[12] The most salient point in Parandowski's creative process, his main literary virtue, so to say, is his search and quest for the truth to which only great writers are pervious.[13]

Another review article by Zofia Starowiejska-Morstinowa called Parandowski "the poet of the great peace," praising his detachment and non-involvement in transitory issues of the day. His book is a successful and well-balanced synthesis of scholarship and fiction; it is by no means anti-Catholic. Although following the footsteps of the Polish positivists of the nineteenth century, Parandowski's work is free from those vestiges of romanticism which often marred their writing, hence his reader feels reality as if with bare hands.[14]

While his works were being discussed and "explained," Parandowski was not idle. There were several projects germinating, but he gave his chief attention to one collection of stories which were partly written before the war, partly during the disastrous years, and a few after the cessation of hostilities. The stories were different in their character and content, yet when they were assembled and the author arbitrarily gave the collection the name *Godzina srodziemnomorska* (The Mediterranean Hour), he noticed that the collection, as in his previous works, constituted an integrated whole. It was, as a Polish critic observed correctly, as if the workshop of the archaeologist and the classical philologist were the Mediterranean basin.[15] The collection is a bridge between the prewar and postwar literary output.

CHAPTER 8

Mediterranean Hour *and* Alchemy of the Word

I Mediterranean Hour

IN the preface to *Mediterranean Hour* Parandowski writes that after assembling this collection of thirteen stories he found that they had something in common, and although written between 1935 and 1949, he could not find a more fitting name for it than the "Mediterranean Hour." Was it escapism, as some readers· claim, or perhaps an assertion of his personality? Was the writer seeking refuge in the past, among those memories which may be, as Bertrand Russell says, either an unbearable burden or a gift of genius no power in the world could destroy? During the horrid, leaden days of occupation the writer, translating Caesar's *De bello civili,* had an encounter with its creator and at some other time Horace made his appearance. Be it as it may, Parandowski's collection again attests to the predominance of the genre of the historical essay, although some of these pieces are simply short stories with cultural and philosophical undertones.

Three Signs of the Zodiac had progressed from the pagan world to Christianity; this collection maintains its boundaries within the limits of the Mediterranean basin; at the same time attaining a general, universal character. It is a hymn to the progress of humanity, a humanity which has an inner need for things beautiful. Particularly evident is this idea in "Lascaux" and "Rozmowa z cieniem" (Conversation with a Shadow). Different in content and the author's treatment of their plots, all thirteen stories have this one unifying idea.

The first tale "Miedzy lampa a switem" is a good example of the method he uses to attune the reader to the general cultural atmosphere of his work.[1] The author sets the tone for his entire collection by introducing a contemporary man reflecting on the history of antiquity which is evoked by concrete objects: in this instance the ancient coins amassed by the numismatist who, talking to the young poet, explains their value and their history, musing like Pushkin's "covetous knight" on how much joy and misery those molecules of the blood of an empire brought in this world. As in previous works, the role of the dialogue is important, although it lapses too often into monologue and inner monologue (the device of a diary) of the erudite numismatist.

Parandowski's hero is no "covetous knight"; hoarding gold is not his purpose, he is only too happy to share his knowledge of his coins with any interested person. A skeptic, a somewhat fatigued and withdrawn man, reminiscent of Chekhov's hero in "The Dreary Story,"[2] his personality is further revealed in the relationship with his wife, a lady of excellent health, impeccable taste, the embodiment of the latest fashion, unburdened by any moral or intellectual doubts. She despises numismatics, but loves money and knows how to use it. In her hands it turns into beautiful dresses, handsome furniture, tasty dishes. According to the laws of juxtaposition, her husband on the other hand exclaims that while showing rare coins to the young poet he felt "centuries ringing in his hand." His wife has sufficient knowledge of the coins to realize their material valule (it helped her to recognize one of the rarest pieces and to convert it into a grand piano). With his usual acidity Parandowski lets his hero state cryptically that this quality is no longer of any assistance to the wife, since all of the rare coins are kept in a special deposit box: to open it forcibly would mean to break down half of the wall in which the box is immured in their apartment.

The story, told in the form of the diary, opens with a specific event on a specific date—the thirteenth of March. This form has a number of advantages: it creates an intimate atmosphere, and within a short span of pages the writer is able to present the contemplative numismatist hinting at his estrangement from his wife, who is entertaining guests just then. The second part begins with the entrance of the young poet and the ensuing demonstration of the coins, each representing a significant and salient point, an historical moment of antiquity. Finally the conversation is interrupted by the appearance of the scholar's wife which serves as a return to modern times and a philosophical excursion "into the last period—the twentieth century,"[3] and final illumination of the relationship between husband and wife as well as an explanation of how the diary came to be written.

The wife's appearance, her way of life, the artificiality and shallowness of culture (she places books around her drawing room in a deliberately disordered fashion although she never reads) is compared by one scholar to a lowly copper coin which even now does not cease to be desired by beggar and statesman alike.[4] The end is a "parenthetical" remark, the author's footnote: "the diary was blank after these words and has probably undergone all the rigors of wartime conditions in a cellar." This short but rich story is probably the most "modern" in its exposition of the personages. The philosophical excursions into history are most credible, since it is the scholar himself who digresses into antiquity.

Most of the other stories, with a few exceptions (particularly "Max von Trott," "Rodecki," and the lyrical "Pokoj wigilijny" (A Room on Christmas Eve) a kind of *Stimmungserzählung* show Parandowski's propensity for the method of "philosophical science fiction,"[5] presenting fantastic situations in a concrete and realistic setting. "Slup milowy" (The Milestone) is perhaps the best example of this type of tale. Its hero is a stone, an immovable object, yet a witness to history. The milestone, endowed with great animus and human compassion as well as perspicacity, sees the carriages and chariots fly by, peasants driving their mules and asses laden with the market produce, petitioners trudging along.

Parandowski, always attentive to fine detail, invariably begins his story with an exact date; "The Milestone" is no exception. It begins with the erection of the milestone on Via Postumia. Those were happy times, the stone was young then and had a beautiful inscription with the names of two Caesars, one of them Marcus Aurelius. One day the stone woke up at the sight of a strange warrior, not a Roman legionnaire, sharpening his spear. The men going by now were strangers, blond and blue-eyed, as were their women who would stop to gaze pensively at the stone. One night one of them secretly came to it and furtively lifting up her skirt sat astride and rubbed her naked pubis against its rough surface. Others followed her, returning later with babies in their arms and flowers with which they adorned the stone in gratitude for their new-found fertility. "But oh wanderer," muses the stone, "it was their youth and beauty and not my magic as they thought, to which they should be indebted."

Time passes, no one takes care of the road and it is no more. The stone has numerous adventures: once it is taken for a boundary marker and it witnessed several generations fighting for a piece of land; another time it is taken for a tomb of Saint Aurelius and is installed in a church as an object of adoration and worship. The times have changed, monks in long frocks are walking by, reminding the stone of the ancient philosophers. After many trials and tribulations the stone's true identity is recognized, and it is installed in a museum.

As in the previous story Parandowski presents a picture of history pivoted on a concrete physical object: the centuries ring from the coins in the hands of a numismatist; in "The Milestone" the object is itself the narrator. We accept the poetical licence of this animism while the stone calmly, epically and yet with lyricism and humor describes the history of Ancient Rome and its environs. This device renders the story extremely compact because the stone is static, the action has to come from the outside, the movement and motion are external. The narrative begins with the apostrophe so common to the epic: "Oh Wanderer! Listen to my story" and ends with "Confess oh wanderer that you did not waste any time in stopping before my putrid remains . . ."; thus in spite of the broad cultural excursion the narrative retains a personal intimate character.

Parandowski's collection deals with a number of problems and the writer treats the material accordingly. Two stories, "Rodecki" and "Max von Trott" present interesting similarities. Each tale bears the name of its hero, each of whom is motivated by a passion for knowledge and a fanatical attachment to an idea and an ideal. Both stories end tragically: Rodecki dies through an accident, Max von Trott destroys himself. The first is at times humorous and optimistic. Rodecki, an old scholar, an incorrigible crank, is absolutely engrossed in antiquity, his interest and scholarly predilections absorb him so completely that at the mature stage of his life he reads almost nothing but the *Corpus inscriptionum latinarum*, his *livre de chevet*. Rodecki is aloof from this world. His only earthly passion is tobacco which he exchanges for *Vini dei castelli romani* when he moves to Rome. During one of his excursions in the catacombs he is lost and never found.

Max von Trott is a brilliant German scholar, a rare combination of physical fitness and beauty with great intelligence and considerable knowledge in archaeology. Yet this young man, who, to use Parandowski's definition, provokes a pagan mist of feminine sensuality to billow on a beach when he goes to take a swim, an idol of women (and what women!) who eagerly submit to him, this paragon is obsessed with the riddle of the earth. Such is his fanatical obsession that, unable to cope with it, he commits suicide.

In comparison with "Rodecki," "Max von Trott" is an infinitely simple story in its narrative, told by a scholar who hears a name pronounced with disrespect, defends it, and proceeds to tell the story of Max von Trott. The narrator knew him personally, frequently talked with him, worked with him and even witnessed his tragic death.

"Rodecki," despite its simple plot, has a complicated exposition, a number of secondary problems, and is one of the best examples of Parandowski's narrative art. From the opening of the story the reader would hardly divine that its hero will be a modest schoolteacher from Poland. A group of five people—two ladies and three gentlemen, returning from Appartamento Borgia go through Galleria Lapidaria. The ladies walk indifferently, like typical tourists, thinking that the objects displayed in a gallery are there to break the monotony of the walk. The men, however, view every object with interest, stopping frequently to discuss certain inscriptions. It is a recurrent theme in Parandowski's work, a peripatetic conversation, an amble through antiquity and the reaction of modern men to it. The conversation is sustained primarily by a scholar, Professor Danielski, who explains to Bartnicki, the secretary of the Polish embassy at the Vatican, the significance and deterioration of straight Roman letters, culminating in the utter ugliness of Gothic script.

After viewing several monuments the company returns to Bartnicki's house. At dinner one of the participants, Dr. Samson, recalls his old Latin teacher, an unusual character, who, when angry, petrified his class by swearing in the Latin at one time

used by Roman legionnaires or exchanged in quarrels by shep-
herds at the Forum Boarium. Professor Danielski also remembers Rodecki, whom he met on several occasions. As the company reminisces, they decide that their old teacher belongs to
the past generation. To everybody's surprise Bartnicki announces
that Rodecki is still alive and lives in Rome, occasionally getting
into trouble and having the embassy bail him out. He is over-
joyed to be in Rome since he knows it by heart from books; and
so conversant is he with every stone in the Forum that he would
love to invite them to a glass of wine. But since it is impossible,
he drinks all by himself. Just as the ladies inquire why he was
never invited to their house, the telephone rings and Bartnicki
returns perturbed with the news he has just heard: Rodecki is
missing in one of the Catacombs.

The construction of "Rodecki" has a drama-like form. The
introduction of the ambiance, physical surroundings, dramatis
personae with a hint of their spiritual development and quest—
this section can be regarded as a prologue. The narrative that
follows, interlaced with various observations and digressions, is
carried by three men who describe Rodecki one after the other,
culminating with Bartnicki's disclosure that the Latin teacher
lives in Rome. At this point, when the reader would expect the
main hero to enter the stage, the story reaches its climax with a
telephone call portending disaster and the epilogue—Parandowski's digression into the tragedy of Rodecki and speculation
about the day of judgment when the hero will appear with
the rest of the Christian martyrs, unknown to them. Rodecki
never actually appears before the reader; he is only talked about.
However, his personality emerges vividly against the carefully
depicted Roman background. The galleries and the gentlemen
are all convincing, and an attractive portrait of Bartnicki's wife
is executed with great plasticity and sentiment. The men's
spiritual and intellectual qualities are also sharply delineated, and
because of their different characters and inclinations, they unfold
Rodecki's personality to the fullest.

Musings and reminiscences are of great import in Parandowski's collection. One of the stories is even called "Rozmyslania
kwietniowe" (April Thoughts) in which the narrative hinges
on a specific date, April 6, with which two historical figures,
Archilochus and Petrarch, whose lives and fates were somewhat

similar, are associated. A few years later this story will grow into another longer study, a biographical work, *Petrarka* (Petrarch). Parandowski's predilection for a reminiscent short story with a general cultural and philosophical foundation is best exemplified in his story entitled "Roscher"[6] named for the encyclopedia which for him was such a source of inspiration (not unsimilar to the tomes Rodecki read) that he personifies it here. Remembrance of things past is all important. In fact the story begins: "Once more the first snow brought with it a memory which had become closely associated with that time of the year, that waking up in the morning under the leaden clouds and hearing the whining of the wind, I could safely say to myself: 'It won't be long before Roscher appears for an hour's chat.' "[7]

The tone of the narrative is set, the writer is in a pensive mood, the past returns: "The memories which come to me with the first snow date back to a grim day in the late autumn when I received from Leipzig two new instalments of the *Ausführliches Lexikon der griechischen und römischen Mythologie.*" The reason for the reflective mood is the last instalment of the *Lexikon;* his treasure is finally assembled and he can "lean back, close his eyes and be lost in thought." The device is not new for Parandowski; it is a philosophical excursion. The *Roscher* appears to the writer as a dear and welcome guest. Mesmerized by memories, the reader hardly perceives the situation as fantastic because the reveries transfer the mind across centuries and space and simultaneously keep it within the boundaries of personal experience.

This is precisely what happens in "Roscher": the writer remembers his childhood, the day when he began to acquire the first volume of the dictionary, the interruptions caused by the First World War and subsequent publication of the further instalments. The lexicon comprises ten volumes, 1,000 pages each. What a rich field for perusal from the modest *Aba* to the omnipotent if at times ridiculous *Zeus.* Since the *Roscher* was compiled over a long period of years, by a number of scholars, it is not uniform in its contents:

Almost all the passions of nineteenth and twentieth century scholars can be found here: some spot agrarian myths everywhere and use this peasant theology to explain gods and rites; others, fascinated by stars, will not rest until they have interpreted every myth with the help of celestial phenomena. There are some who derive the whole of Olympus from India, and their articles are full of Sanskrit. There is also a moment of pan-Babylonian mania, to which "Roscher" owes some interesting passages on the religions of Mesopotamia. On other occasions it is Egypt that gets the upper hand, and everything tends to prove that the gods of Greece were born in the shadow of the Pyramids. And there are lovers with new-fangled ideas from those days when anthropology turned the philologists' heads—adherents of that "Botokudenphilologie," as Wilamowitz-Moelledorf used to describe it, worshippers of taboos, totems, fetishes . . .[8]

Reminiscences and ruminations give birth to new memories of personal experiences and digressions. Parandowski reflects on monotheistic theory, remembering his conversation at Olympia with a Japanese scholar.[9] The story ends with the evocation of the old times and lyrical and nostalgic chords:

Good old "Roscher." I like it both for its virtues and vices. It is systematic and chaotic, serious and frivolous. During its fifty years of life it let itself be carried away by all kinds of passion, and collected a huge amount of erudition much of which smells of old-fashioned prejudice. It looks a little like the diary of a woman who had many lovers and swore eternal love to each of them. And, as from such a diary, a faint perfume of love rises from these severe pages, covered with small print: the men who passed here genuinely loved their old texts and even older gods and, in their admiration, erred with the fanaticism of the faithful. How I miss you, my good companion!

The final lines, the colophon of the story, explain why the *Roscher* is no more:

W. H. Roscher's fellow-countrymen entered my house in the autumn of 1944 to set it on fire. They performed the work of destruction with the same thorough care and the same obstinacy which accompany their nation in any work. A friend of mine, who visited my home at the end of January 1945, saw the burnt library. Whole rows of books had kept their shape. These ashen ghosts collapsed when touched! *Roscher* was there, more monumental than the others. A snowstorm which broke in through the shattered windows seized it and swept it away.[10]

In "Lascaux" Parandowski uses the technique later to be known as "multiple selective omniscience." Here too, the harsh reality is interrupted by memories. The writer resting in Swider hears that the son of his subtenant has been arrested by the Germans, and at the same time thinks about the children playing and discovering at Lascaux the marvellous cave with the prehistoric paintings. The contrast is striking: despite the sad news and his dark dejection, he yet evokes the human spirit, effervescent, creative, and reaching for the stars. Here, Parandowski presciently expresses Csokor's somewhat pessimistic and reconciliatory exclamation: "Der Mensch ist in der Kloake geboren, stirbt in der Kloake, aber inzwischen hat er die Möglichkeit nach den Sternen zu greifen." (Man was born in a cloaca, and dies in a cloaca, but in between he has the possibility of reaching for the stars).[11] How much more optimistic is Parandowski's attitude which recognizes human frailties and proclivities yet still affirms the sanity of *homo sapiens;* all this on a sad September day of 1940.

"Spotkanie wsrod gwiazd" (An Encounter among Stars) is an imaginary dialogue between Caesar and Cicero, a conversation based on their own reminiscences as well as "acquired" knowledge of modern times. Patterned on the dialogues of Lucian, it reviews the history and culture of ancient Rome.

"Rozmowa z cieniem" (A Conversation with a Shadow) is a far more impressive and ambitious dialogue between Piotr (Parandowski's favorite name)—a modern man—and Horace. The Roman poet appears to Piotr at dusk in the shape of a shadow, a fantastic situation but rendered credible by the author's presentation of it as a reverie.

The poet, respecting and admiring the ancients, points out that times have progressed since the Aristotelian theory of the three unities in literature. Many new means have been discovered to create beauty. Dante and Shakespeare created a multiple world of good and evil, of ambition and compassion, of love and hatred. To Horace's remarks that such a poet would create disorder and be obliged to seek pearls in a dungheap, Piotr calmly replies: "Just as in life." And to Horace's indignant: "Since when does poetry have to seek justification in life?" he points to the stagnation of poetry whose creators rigidly cling to the established canons. Kochanowski's Latin poetry has withered with time but his Polish verses gave him immortality. The innate drive of man brought him to creativity and daring experimentation; he possessed the intuition necessary to sustain him in art long before he learned how to plow a field or breed cattle ("Lascaux"). The romanticists "opened up the collar" of their poetry to breathe freely. In Poland they became the prophets and the conscience of the nation, blessing the martyrs and calling the people to fight against tyranny.

The modern man and Horace complement each other in their intellectual and cultural make-up. Horace, with the wisdom of the ancients, has the last word as he consoles Piotr about the fears and anxieties common to every generation. Every poet is primarily a poet of his time and nation. There is no necessity to fear a lack of originality or a repetition of the same verses. Word combinations are uncountable, sufficient for many lives of one person. Nor should one fear the avalanche of books created every day—the plow was invented to satisfy hunger, and evanescent poetry is created to satiate the hunger for beauty. To Piotr's anguished exclamation that the machine age destroys the world of Phidias and Polyclete as well as that of Raphael, Horace replies that each generation was plagued by the same anxieties. Only one question remains unanswered: what is the world all about? The shadow replies that it is impossible to speak about celestial things with ordinary words. The riddle of existence remains unresolved. Using the form of a dialogue, Parandowski again establishes a synthesis between the modern and the old, permitting him to see life not only from the contemporary point of view but *sub specie aeternitatis*.

Parandowski returns to a more conventional form, although the dialogue is still important, in "Godzina srodziemnomorska" (The Mediterranean Hour) bearing the same name as his entire collection. In this, one of his most captivating stories, he creates a novel and original literary device by boldly confronting a writer, Joseph Conrad, with a character from one of Conrad's novels. The personality of Conrad is an enigma, the fascination and pride of the Polish nation. It has an additional significance for Parandowski; Conrad's works transcend national boundaries and acquire universal meaning with the starting point of "the blue level of the Mediterranean, the charmer and the deceiver of audacious man . . ." as he described it in *The Rover*. Parandowski wrote about and mentioned Conrad several times in his works. We remember young "Korzeniowski (Conrad)" in "The

Alliance with the Sea." In a collection of *Visits and Encounters* (Part II) Parandowski included "Conrad," a lengthy essay of informative character written in 1948, and in the story "An Ordinary Day," from the collection *September Night*, the writer, depicting an evening during the German occupation of Warsaw in an apartment of Aniela Zagórska, Conrad's translator, described how reminiscences about the Pole who was a great English writer helped the company to escape the oppressive reality. Parandowski's preoccupation with Conrad, who must have been a source of inspiration to him as a perennial Odysseus visiting exotic lands (there is always an undercurrent of romanticism in Parandowski's works), led the writer to baptize his older son Zbigniew Konrad, with Conrad's translator, Aniela Zagórska, for a godmother. By Parandowski's own admission Conrad fascinated him as a person, and influenced Parandowski's later, more mature prose.[12]

The beginning of the story has a realistic setting: Conrad rests with his wife in a hotel on the coast of Corsica. The searing sun forces all the guests to retreat from the garden, and the writer remains alone looking at the blue Mediterranean. Suddenly to his vexation he beholds the magnificent old man, Peyrol, from his novel, *The Rover*. The pirate walks up to his creator just as he appears in the novel; dressed in . . . "white shirt, a short blue jacket with metal buttons and a high rolled collar, a pair of white trousers which he fastened with a red bandana handkerchief by way of a belt. With a black, shiny low-crowned hat on his head he made a very creditable prizemaster."[13] "Luckily," states Parandowski, "there were no passers-by around at that moment . . . otherwise he would attract a crowd."[14] Then a conversation, not unlike the "conversation with a shadow," begins. Having thus confronted the two men Parandowski proceeds with an argument between the writer and his hero who, once created, claims the right to an unchangeable and independent existence. Peyrol feels that his *raison d'être* is justified; he is unwilling to appear in any of the novels from the Napoleonic age which Conrad intended to write. His existence was logical, just as his death was consequential and justified. His sacrifice was neither for Arlette, nor for Real; he died for France.

Thus Parandowski presents an interesting variation on the old theme of the confrontation between an author and a character

he has created. Parandowski has of course often dealt with
this theme, particularly in connection with the writing of his
Heaven in Flames; Grodzicki often acted the way he wanted and
not the way Parandowski wanted him to act. In "The Mediterranean Hour" he goes beyond this perennial theme, forcing the
writer and his hero to discuss this very problem. Furthermore,
Peyrol, although claiming that he loves his creator, has certain
misgivings about Conrad. His love for the English language, his
inability or unwillingness to write about Poland are strange to
Peyrol. Conrad defends his position by pointing to the vagaries of
art, its whimsical and almost mysterious process, incomprehensi-
ble to hardened Peyrol, although art was his mother and the
writer his real father. The end is a reconciliatory note: Conrad
realizes that by creating heroes like Peyrol, alive and immortal,
he gives part of himself away. Peyrol seems to comprehend.
When the writer opens his eyes, blinded by the sun, the Roman
profile of the pirate is no longer above him.

The collection concludes with a strange story, an expertly
executed pirouette and literary exercise, the most baffling and
teasing and at the same time, the most challenging of all Parandowski's works. Referring to an incident in Book Eleven of the
Odyssey, the writer raises a metaphysical question: What is
reality? He then paints a generic picture of the Mediterranean
Basin and of Odysseus, a symbol of searching humanity. The
encounter of Odysseus and Proteus, whose main characteristic
is the ability to change his shape, poses a question to the hero:
How real is reality? Proteus proves conclusively that Odysseus'
experience is transcendental and his role in art is somewhat
ambiguous. Is he as human as the world is led to believe, or a
bundle of words, a bundle which contains a germ of independent
existence? Is it not true that each generation saw in *the Odyssey*
something different, altering its perception of the hero, changing
its attitude as Proteus would change his shape?[15]

Nothing is real, not even the desert-like landscape surrounding
Proteus and Odysseus, for all of a sudden it changes although
the two see different picture. Proteus, wiser than the sage Theban
Tiresias, beholds the city in which Odysseus and Telemachus
wander, as in a modern *Ulysses,* unknown to beholders, bearing
different names. Telemachus wears glasses. Tiresias sees Penelope's dream, although her name is not Penelope. Odysseus admits

to have become wiser on Proteus' "shores of non-existence" and gaily walks away with "the dawn like a dog running after him."

II Alchemy of the Word

In *The Mediterranean Hour*, written over a period of several years, questions about the problems of the writer, his function in society and life are a recurring theme. These questions constantly preoccupy Parandowski; we remember that even his earliest works deal with the spiritual and creative processes of the writer. He was specifically interested in a writers' laboratory, his workshop and in the mysterious and fascinating processes of literary creation.

This persistent interest led him to *Alchemia słowa* (Alchemy of the Word) which began as a modest lecture but after many years and adventures appeared in 1950 in book form. The writer himself describes the emergence of the book in a preface to its second edition in 1955. We shall have to return to his prewar years, the period when he was editor of *Pamietnik Warszawski* (Warsaw Review).

Around 1930 Parandowski was asked to present a lecture in Wilno, at one of the literary Thursdays. The writer was not sure what topic he should choose, until suddenly he was dazzled by the idea of speaking about the creative processes of a writer. Dazzled was the word, stressed Parandowski, and he was right, for he received a cordial and warm reception for his "pogawedka" (informal talk). Although busy with this periodical, he was able to go to Wilno in November when it was cold there and staying in a cell of the former Basilian monastery near the *Ostra Brama* (an old city gate with a miraculous icon), he saw and relived the mood and the ghosts of Mickiewicz's "Improvisation" from his *Forefathers' Eve*—a masterpiece which, among other things, dealt with the fate of the great poet and his fellow students. Parandowski later returned to this incident in his essay on Mickiewicz:

Mickiewicz wrote *Konrad Wallenrod* in Russia. He was living then in enforced residence in 1824 after the trial of the Philomaths. These were an association of university youth at Vilna, and the poet . . . was the soul of it. Senator Novosiltsev . . . had the leading spirit of the movement imprisoned. Mickiewicz, shut up in a cell of the Basilian monastery heard the November wind blowing and howling as a background to his lonely meditations."[16]

After the lecture in Wilno Parandowski could see how right he was in selecting such a topic, for his presentation was followed by a vigorous discussion. Other lectures followed with the same result, each audience manifesting great interest and enthusiasm, thus the compilation of notes grew in scope and size. Parandowski always intended to reorganize them but other and more compelling work, first the *Olympic Discus* and then *Heaven in Flames*, forced him to shelve the project. Once Parandowski caught himself subconsciously jotting down everything that pertained to the creative processes of a writer. Soon he put all of his notes in a separate folder, which as time progressed began to bulge.

The outbreak of the war put a stop to the growth in his lecture notes, but he returned to them in the grim year of 1941 when he began to reorganize his material and turn it into what he thought would be a little book of about a hundred and twenty pages. On moving from Warsaw Parandowski took these notes, fortunately, for had they stayed behind they would have met the fate of the rest of his papers. After the war the notes accompanied Parandowski on his travels to Sweden, Norway and France, increasing visibly after each trip to the Royal Library in Stockholm and the Bibliothèque Nationale in Paris.

When Parandowski returned to Poland he used the notes as the basis for a one year comparative literature lecture course at the Catholic University in Lublin. This was an important milestone in their life; each chapter (lecture) was reorganized and augmented and carefully thought over. Suddenly the spring wind blew over these pages, and Parandowski began to publish fragments from his study in various periodicals, fashioning each article according to the occasion and the wishes of the publisher. Thus when he finally decided to publish his study in book form, he saw that all these published fragments, lacking continuity, did not constitute an integrated whole. The summer vacations at Ustka remain in Parandowski's memory as periods devoted to "sewing" up of *disiecta membra* of the *Alchemy of the Word*.

These long adventures and peregrinations finally ended in the autumn of 1950 when the lectures appeared in print. Immediately popular, the book was sold out within a short time and became a bibliographical rarity. Readers and critics began to clamor for another edition but Parandowski was too occupied with other works to devote time to its republication. After a thorough revision and augmentation, his *Alchemy of the Word* appeared again in 1956.

The special flavor and varied contents of this volume were indicated in 1958 in a review by the present writer:

The author, endowed with great erudition, unfolds a fascinating picture of all aspects of creation and of the problems that faced the writer from time immemorial: calling, inspiration, dedication, vision, power of observation, the role of women in a writer's life, his workshop, various objects that surround him, and their importance in the creative process. Actual work is amply discussed, including the role of stimulants, alcohol, and tobacco. It is a long chain of incidents without being monotonous, all brilliantly told and beautifully written. It is a kaleidoscopic picture of schools and ideas, a pondering on the magic of the word and the secrets of the trade, with the appeal to foster and study the language. Without aspiring to be a literary study, *per se*, the book touches upon the history of literary ideas by treating Aristotle's *Poetics*, the *Letters* of Horace, Longinus with his presumed treatise, Boileau's *Art poétique*, and Dmochowski's *Sztuka rytmotworcza*.

The chapters on style and "From the First Thought to the Last" are perhaps the most brilliant, astounding in their lucidity of style and amazing perspicacity. As the author asserts, this volume is not an autobiographical work, nor is it a hidden memoir; it has not been intended as a textbook for future "geniuses," but rather as an introduction for the layman into the intricacies of the emergence of a book and various facets of the life and habits of a writer which are vitally important and of which the reader often has not the slightest idea.[17]

The material gathered by Parandowski is of Gargantuan scope, but writing with verve and passion, he was able to retain his literary equilibrium. The work is by no means incondite but a well-constructed series of historio-literary essays.

CHAPTER 9

The Sundial

W przedziwnym mieszkam ogrodzie,
Gdzie zyja kwiaty i dzieci
I gdzie po slonca zachodzie
Usmiech nam z oczu swieci.

—Leopold Staff

THE early years of the 1950's were a period of prolific literary activity in Parandowski's life. In 1950 he gave up his position as a professor of comparative literature at the Lublin Catholic University in order to devote all his energy and time to writing. The time spent at Lublin had been profitable for the writer: he furthered his knowledge of antiquity and of Western literature, the preparation for his lectures resulted in the publication of *Alchemy of the Word* and *Petrarch*.

Meanwhile he did not neglect his duties as President of the Polish PEN Club, traveling extensively in this capacity. One such trip was particularly significant for the writer. In 1949 he attended The PEN congress held in Venice. There Parandowski walked again the old streets of the city and the island of Grado which he had known so well as a child. This trip—perhaps combined with a desire to escape from the contradictory reality of the beginning of the 1950's in Poland, his persistent preoccupation with the past coupled with the search for a new mode of expression—led the writer to a curious work, *The Sundial,* which again upon its completion was hailed as a modern Polish classic.

As in many instances before, the book was a by-product of some other literary endeavor. In this case the writer created a number of stories from his childhood while resting from the toils of the translation of Homer's *Odyssey.*[1] The work, typically for Parandowski, augmented and enlarged, as he progressed, followed a traditional West-European pattern. Certain echoing of Tolstoy and Chekhov are discernible in it, but it is precisely

119

because of its hackneyed theme that it deserves our attention. Parandowski created a masterpiece of unsurpassed originality, freshness and vigor.

Parandowski's new book—*Zegar sloneczny* (The Sundial) does not deal with the subject of antiquity, nor does it have anything to do with gnomonics. To draw a guarded parallel, it is rather like a *Charakterroman*, like Otto Flake's *Die Sanduhr;* yet the similarity shoud not be exaggerated. The essence of *The Sundial* may be explained by a congratulatory statement at the celebration of Parandowski's fiftieth anniversary of creative activity: "Oby zegar Jego zycia byl zawsze sloneczny!" This of course is a play on words, for "Sloneczny" in Polish is an adjective, meaning "sunny," thus the sentence in English: "May the clock of your life be always sunny (unclouded)." The subject Parandowski turned to was his carefree and unclouded childhood. The topic is not new; Polish literature frequently treats it and Parandowski himself dealt with it in his *Heaven in Flames.*

The Sundial is not preoccupied with any specific problem. Writing about his own life, Parandowski does not create an ordinary autobiography. His book is a collection of seemingly detached stories; yet all of it forms an inseparable whole.

Any writer reconstructing the childhood of a hero, particularly when the hero happens to be the writer himself, has to contend with several problems. Does he reminisce about his childhood and see it through the eyes of an experienced adult, or does he try to recreate events as the child saw them at the time of their occurrence? Tolstoy attempted to do the latter in his *Childhood,* but he was too preoccupied with the inner dialectics of an infant, thus his work, bearing the traces of his own life, is a conscious effort to move away from personal experience and to create a universal, but at the same time specific hero. Tolstoy and Gorki recreate the lives of the heroes chronologically; both use a certain starting point. In Tolstoy's work it is a specific morning and in Gorki's *Childhood* it is the death of his father. James Joyce goes further, he "remembers" the first physical sensations of a young child. In spite of the flowing narrative, each of the instants in Tolstoy's and Gorki's works is vividly projected which is not surprising, for what is childhood for any grown-up man but a number of bright flashes of memory, some more distinct than others?

Parandowski recognized this and created a number of stories with a particular incident as a central point. This is an extremely specious device, because our memory is not a continuous narrative. To add a greater verisimilitude, Parandowski begins his stories by presenting a specific occurrence in his own family. The very first story "The Bullfinch" is a good example. Piotr, Parandowski's son, learns how to read, and struggling with his ABC's, experiences a moment of triumph, when seemingly disjointed letters form a word, a concept known to the little boy. Immediately after, the author uses the device of reminiscence and evocation and moves into his own childhood. This constant projection from the present life of a grown man into the past, evoked by the observance of his own children, gives the book intimate character. Using separate incidents makes it a series of flashes of retrospection and memory. Parandowski remembers but does not muse, and creates an impressionistic painting with a realistic foundation.

The *Sundial* begins with Parandowski's earliest impressions and ends with what was officially considered the conclusion of one's childhood: graduation from secondary school. He is too sophisticated to reflect on his pre-natal experiences or the experiences similar to James Joyce's child. The writer, rather, begins by presenting himself at a time when he began to react intelligently to people and events around him. The starting point, just as in Tolstoy's *Childhood* is a certain incident with associations surrounding it. Tolstoy's hero is too analytical, and therefore his work acquires somewhat fantastic dimensions, because a child can feel but can hardly reason as can an adult, and least of all could he put his experiences on paper. The reader is imperceptibly forced to accept this liberty and poetic licence.

Parandowski's device of memories and evocations saves him from pitfalls in the depiction of his hero. The construction of his work is based on observations, memory and juxtaposition (but not on contrast) of his experiences with those of his children. Once the story has introduced Piotr, Zbyszek or Roma, the writer abruptly reverts to his own childhood, and the narrative acquires a studiedly naïve tone, although often it is interrupted by the author's own digression, or is interlaced with the tales of his grandmother, his neighbors or some relatives, but always by grown-ups. The stories therefore are narrated by

Parandowski the writer, Parandowski the child and by other personages in the collection. This device gives the autobiographical work a wider scope, and aside from personal memories, unfolds the picture of Lwow in the beginning of the twentieth century. In spite of these digressions, events progress in a chronological order.

It is interesting to note how imperceptibly the naïve tone of the narrative changes as the child grows up. Again a parallel would be useful: like the hero in Tolstoy's *Trilogy* who does not have to rely on the "fenestration" device, but considers his surroundings and the people analytically, Parandowski's hero relies less and less on the digressions of Parandowski the writer and consciously remembers his schooldays, its pranks, joys and sorrows.

It should be borne in mind that this book is not a flowing biography, but rather a collection of twenty-two separate stories. This peculiar construction is important for several reasons: apart from a short-story technique at which the writer is obviously adept, it has important ramifications in regard to the plausibility of the child's memories. Separately, each story is an incident in the hero's life; taken together they paint a complete canvas of life seen through the eyes of a growing boy.

Although the story "Tableau" would seem the obvious one to end the cycle, it is significant that the author does not place it last. It deals with the arrangement for a group picture of the graduating class, the farewell dinner with a nocturnal walk of the students at the dawn of a new life. The boys realize that the world they are leaving behind seemed unjust and rigid at times, yet the world they are entering with such fortitude and optimism will be fraught with conflicts which are harder to resolve. The book ends on a less melancholy note—the writer's inner monologue, addressed to his daughter Roma. In the "Lullaby," Parandowski, observing the little girl, thinks of his childhood and about ancient Rome (hence the name Roma) and its culture; the melancholy of the "Tableau" is broken. The "Lullaby" has another function in this collection. In the first story we recall it was the writer's youngest son Piotr who evoked Parandowski's memories of his childhood. In the last it is the oldest child who serves the same literary function. The sundial of life has run its course to begin another cycle in this ever-continuing life.

The last story, like the rest of the cycle, is in a minor key.
The writer, for a long time impervious to music, concludes his
work with an adagio which ends with a soporific whisper.[2]
Without resorting to the form of a novel, Parandowski presents
a panoramic picture of his native city by creating a gallery of
types, by consistent poetic digression, and by generous and free
insertion of the legends and tales of the large provincial city.
In this he is somewhat similar to Prus, although his description
is necessarily more intimate and personal. The characters appear
and reappear, which makes them more alive and prominent.

Parandowski's grandmother made an indelible impression upon
him—an impression which is evident in *Sundial*. The book begins
with this majestic personality who reached the venerable age
of ninety-eight, and it ends with an allusion to her, although the
reader is aware that she died some time before. One touching
story, "The Phonograph," especially concerns her. This was an
age when the phonograph was a rarity, and the new machine
was approached with great curiosity. Everybody tried to say
a few words into the microphone. When it was grandmother's
turn, she bravely began: 'If it is true that my voice will be
recorded . . . when I am no longer here . . .'" and finished her
statement by blessing everybody at which Parandowski's uncle
took out a white handkerchief, and his mother burst into tears.
Some time later, when the grandmother was no longer with
them, the boy's mother found the record and played it back; a
soothing and consoling moment helping to retain not only the
voice but her personality.

The grandmother's personality was indeed unusual. A somewhat rigid and authoritarian woman of fixed principles with a
cryptic and abrupt style, not devoid of certain prejudices and at
times superstitious, she was a charming and kind person. She
lived in a world of her own; she remembered vividly the uprising of 1830, and stories of her father who participated in the
Napoleonic wars. Berating somebody, she would refer to him
as a "squirt," a greenhorn, forgetting that the greenhorn in
question might be seventy years old. When hiring a coach she
would put forth a number of conditions: the coachman was to
drive slowly, under no circumstances was he to beat the horses
and he was to be paid twelve crowns for the trip, the last being
the most grievous stipulation. The coachman, a huge peasant

sitting on the coachbox of his cab, would beat his chest with his fist the size of a small cabbage and haggle. "Antek," the grandmother would sternly address him in the diminutive, looking into his red face with a big mustache on it, "the wrath of the Lord be upon you! Have you forgotten how your father would drive me down for six when you ate all of my candies?" The coachman would jump off, kiss the grandmother's hand and help her and her grandson into the carriage. The grandmother was indulgent towards her grandson, and he often sought her protection from his outwardly stern mother.

The mother's portrait is one of the most magnificent and appealing of Parandowski's creation. Taking into account the difference between the visual and literary art, she can be compared to one of Murillo's Madonnas. The writer achieves a portrait of her spiritual qualities by refraining from depicting her physical portrait. He simply states at certain times that she was very beautiful. This device is consistent because a child would see a total picture of his mother, rather than depict her beauty. What is of consequence is what her son feels, how he reacts to her actions. In this Parandowski is a master, he creates a personal and yet such an abstract mother, close to the child as only a mother could be, at the same time distant; a portrait of intimate and unattainable divinity. The boy must have been very close to his mother, perhaps partly because his father died when he was two years old. There is only one reference to him in the entire collection. The mother's personality is further revealed in her relationship to other people and particularly to Parandowski's uncle. Strict and at times stern, although infinitely gentle with the child, she is soft-hearted in helping her brother out of many financial quandaries.

Parandowski's uncle is a squanderer and a crank. The collection abounds in other cranks, humorous and witty, at times pathetic and sad. Some are itinerants like Tolstoy's Grisha in his *Childhood*. Some are what is known as "superfluous people" in literature. At times the downtrodden met their demise as a result of unrequited love or some other passion, and sometimes they are just ordinary misfits like Lolo (in the story of the same name), or the poor and the insulted like Grzegorz in the story "Return of the Fairytales."

The Sundial is bright and warm, optimistic, and to borrow a classical term, a comedy. Recreating his happy childhood the writer shows subtle psychological tact and presents a realistic, at times sad, but bright, picture of his native city. The most important and striking feature of the collection is the style and the language at which he always excels. Parandowski's language is a superb example of the best Polish prose, it is a colorful, racy, articulate vehicle. The speech of every character is highly individual; be it the language of his mother, of his grandmother, of his uncle or later on, the language of his teachers. The writer skillfully reconstructs the vernacular of the petit bourgeois, the pedestrian hero in the street, of the simple and the wise. Had he never written more than *The Sundial*, Parandowski would always be remembered for his simple and happy masterpiece.

CHAPTER 10

Classics, Collections, and Critics

IN the 1950's Parandowski undertook a number of projects which once again pointed to his scholarly predilection. All of the projects had long histories; the writer thought about them for years and in the case of some, for decades.

In his *Alchemy of the Word* Parandowski had advocated the creation of a school for future writers (not at all such a preposterous idea as some critics thought). Now he energetically supported the establishment of a translators' association which would further the interests and protect the toilers of this misunderstood and often misused profession. In the 1930's a proposal to create a translators' union and to co-ordinate its work with that of the International PEN had been met by a blank wall of indifference. H. G. Wells remarked at one of the meetings that it was not up to the writers' association to worry about these literary craftsmen. Now, because of Parandowski's initiative and persistent efforts, the Polish PEN Club organized between 1950 and 1953 three series of translators' symposia in which various writers participated and which resulted in the publication of an excellent volume *The Art of Translating*. Edited by Michal Rusinek, the book was published in Polish with summaries in French, Russian and English. It covered a wide range of subjects from: "On Theories of Translation in the Past" by Waclaw Borowy, "On Antique Prose" by Kazimierz Kumaniecki, to "Translators' Copyright" by Rusinek. Parandowski participated with several articles.[1]

Parandowski's interest in the art of translating was by no means of a detached, administrative nature. He never shunned the menial work of a "literary craftsman," and his first translation dates back to 1923. Although Parandowski shows a preference for the authors of antiquity (Longus, Caesar, Theophilactus

Simocata), amongst his translations can be found Romain Rolland's *Danton*, Théophile Gautier's *Le Club des Haschischins*, Henry de Montherlant's *Le Bestiaire* (which anticipates Ernest Hemingway's treatment of the bullfights), H. G. Wells' *A Short History of the World* and many others. His most important achievement was the translation of the *Odyssey*. Homer always had a certain fascination for Parandowski; his second article at the beginning of his career was "On the Immortality of Homer."[2] In 1930 he published *Wojna trojanska* (The Trojan War), and in 1935 *Przygody Odyseusza* (The Adventures of Odysseus)—both popularizations for young people of the *Iliad* and the *Odyssey*.

"Translating Homer is an ambition of every European literature":[3] Thus Parandowski began one of his essays describing the history of various translations of Homer's works. The first was executed by Livius Andronicus in the third century B.C. enriching Roman literature. From that time on, with the notable exception of the Middle Ages, every nation in every century tried its hand at it, sometimes producing works which in themselves are monuments of literary endeavor. The most important are Voss's translation into German, and the well-known one by Alexander Pope into English. Poland was no exception. The first Polish translation of Homer was of a fragment of the *Iliad*, rendered by Kochanowski. There were numerous other translators subsequently, among them Szmurla, Popiel, Mleczka, Czubek, and the very popular Siemienski. Joseph Wittlin began his translation of the *Odyssey* in 1914, making it his life-long work. His first edition appeared in 1924, and showed a great indebtedness to Wyspianski.

Unlike Wittlin's translation of the *Odyssey*, written in unrhymed hexameters, Parandowski's translation was rendered in prose. He himself gave the reason for his choice in *Homeryckie boje*. We shall quote the synopsis of his article published in the *Art of Translating*:

The translation is made in prose, a very rare specimen in Polish literature, where poetry is usually translated in verse. According to the author, the latter method did great harm to the original. Some translators made use of the rhymed thirteen-syllabic verse, which has the same meaning as the alexandrine in French poetry; others used the hexameter. The use of rhymed verse forced translators to leave out some of the most important details, to change the mood of the original and the meaning of particular words or even of the content itself. On the other hand, the hexameter sounds strange in Polish, evoking the sensation of monotony which is hard to bear; its use causes also the inevitable deviation from the original text. The most important advantage of a prose translation is that nothing is left out of Homer's original text. This enables the translator to convey the specific atmosphere of the original with all its wealth of detail, to give the reader a clear and readable book. It is only this kind of translation which can show the narrative qualities of the *Odyssey*, the prototype of the novel. The author has given up all attempts at archaism, considering it to be an unnecessary burden, for the use of which no justification can be found.[4]

In response to the publication of Parandowski's translation, Joseph Wittlin, a poet *par excellence*, objected that poetry must be translated into poetry. However, an outstanding Polish poet, the dean of Polish letters, Kazimierz Wierzynski, stated that notwithstanding the excellence of Wittlin's rendering, Parandowski's prose translation is more accurate and precise.[5] We might add that this prose is so rhythmical and majestic as to be poetry itself. The writer spent considerable time working conscientiously on his translation. Also typical of Parandowski is the fact that he began to write a study of Homer. From his modest "On Translating Homer" he progressed to an exhaustive essay, which he used as a preface to his translation, and was toying with the idea of publishing a monograph.[6]

I *Petrarch*

With an allusion to Homer, Parandowski concluded another book, this time about a great humanist whose death fulfilled his temporal wishes—*vivendi scribendique unus finis* (living and writing have the same purpose). Petrarch died reading and studying the *Odyssey*.

In his *Praca nad Petrarka* (Work on Petrarch),[7] Parandowski reported that Petrarch's name was known to him since his early youth when he visited Italy and bought a little volume of Petrarch's sonnets. From that time on "like the tercets of the *Divine Comedy*, the marble plaque on the corners of the streets in Florence, and various streets and piazzas of Milan or Bologna resounded with Petrarch's verse" in Parandowski's memory. In his course on humanism at Lublin Catholic University, his first lecture was on Petrarch. After the stifling and horrid war years the new professor wanted to "breathe fresh air of optimism and faith in man." Eight years later, looking over his notes, he decided to write a monograph. The very next day the die was cast; he concluded a contract with a publishing house. The choice of the topic of Petrarch and his times had important ramifications for Parandowski's re-evaluation of Poland's first postwar years and her future destiny. Coupled with his interest in humanism were Parandowski's musings about the fate of mankind after the cataclysm of the Second World War.

The study on Petrarch is a lengthy, somewhat monotonous essay, a *vie romancée* in which the historical setting is extremely important. Parandowski recreates the epoch at the dawn of humanism and the political upheavals in Italy. The book opens during a civil war in Florence between the Guelphs and the Ghibellines with Petrarch's parents fleeing the city with Dante Alighieri, who was condemned to die at the stake. The family stopped at Arezzo, and it was here that the future poet, humanist, thinker, advocate of the unification of Itlay, the first *uomo universale*, was born. His family moved to Avignon when the young boy was nine years old. After his university studies, Petrarch settled in that city, an important cultural center as well as the residence of the popes. Life in Avignon was carefree for the gilded youth, and Petrarch, who became an intimate and close friend of the powerful Colonna family, although an ordained priest, plunged into its worldly pleasures.

In 1327 the poet met Laura, who became for him what Beatrice was for Dante, "lady beautiful," an inspiration and a recipient of homage in his numerous sonnets. The love was unrequited and this probably led Petrarch to move to the solitary Vaucluse nearby. The protection of the Colonnas and his literary fame secured several sinecures for Petrarch. Various cities and courts began to vie for his presence and sought his help as an ambassador. Petrarch travelled a great deal and, as Parandowski pointed out, was one of the first poets to commune with nature and express his sentiment in verse. His ability to express the intensity of his feeling has been surpassed only by Rousseau. Invited by Paris, Naples and Rome to become Poet Laureate, Petrarch chose Rome and was crowned there in 1341.

He always regarded Rome as the center of European civilization, and urged the popes to return to it. A creator of modern Italian poetry, Petrarch was an enthusiastic admirer of the antiquity which he attempted to reconcile with the Christian doctrine. (Petrarch followed attentively and sympathetically the spectacular career of Cola Rienzi. When the latter was delivered to the Holy Inquisition and put in *Carcer honestus et curialis*, the poet did not reply to the pleas of Rienzi and did not help in his release from the incarceration.) Recognized as a great poet laureate, famous but not affluent, he died at Arqua over the newly translated *Odyssey*.

Presenting a detailed account of Petrarch's life, Parandowski did not give a vast biography nor a literary analysis of the poet's work. Rather, he sketched the salient points in the life and creative activity of the great humanist. It was all the easier since Petrarch left voluminous correspondence in which he consciously tried to depict his own portrait. In this he was a precursor of many who indulged in epistolary art in the seventeenth and eighteenth centuries. Considerable space was devoted to Petrarch's musings, another one of Parandowski's favorite devices, also made easy by the poet's voluminous marginalia. Petrarch, at one time, was interested in the confessions of St. Augustine and some stylistic peculiarities of the confessions are discernible, skillfully deployed, in Parandowski's work. On the whole, Parandowski's style is that of a chronicler, a calm narrator of a *gaweda*. It was not so much the personality of Petrarch and his times, but his way of life and his literary output which fascinated Parandowski. Hence, his preoccupation and liking for a travelogue and epistolary writings. Petrarch appealed to Parandowski as a prototype of the Renaissance man and perhaps because of this he is somewhat schematic, although Parandowski surrounded him with vital historical characters.

It may also be that, notwithstanding his warm relationship and friendship with Boccaccio and others, Petrarch's personality was somewhat detached and abstract; this view may be exaggerated by the paucity of information about him. The same can be said about his love for Laura, an ephemeral, fugitive and yet non-volatile (some scholars believed that she never really existed) divine personality, which in no way impeded Petrarch from begetting children with a robust, georgic woman. Parandowski, the historian, was alert to Petrarch's political aspirations, and refused to treat them with a detached coolness. Indeed he seems to draw a parallel between the fourteenth century and modern times and to point to the supremacy of the Latin world and culture as opposed to the uncouth Teutonic civilization.

The anxieties of Petrarch who meditated about the destiny of Italy and was "the first man to cogitate over her ruin" must have struck a responsive chord among the Poles, who saw their country destroyed and torn by an internecine strife. The problem of the uprooted and of the émigrés must have touched a raw nerve in those of whom Dante said:

> Thou shalt by sharp experience be aware
> How salt the bread of strangers is, how hard
> The up and down of someone else's stair . . .

(Paradiso, XVII—58-60, Transl., Dorothy L. Sayers and Barbara Reynolds, Penguin Books, 1962.)

That is why Parandowski's book was warmly received by the Poles living abroad.[8]

Parandowski's most important achievement lies in the vivid and picturesque depiction of historical Paris, Avignon, Naples and Rome. Parandowski is a master at presenting "the age and the body" of the place. Who could forget the colorful crowds in Avignon, the plague, horrid and fascinating, or the sad end of Cola di Rienzi among the ruins of Rome? The writer feels very much at home in Italy, France or in the snowcapped Alps, where Petrarch felt the presence of God. Parandowski acquires and conveys a cosmic perception of the world and of the whole of modern literature beginning with Dante and concluding with the gentle verses of Slowacki reverberating in their white, crystalline magnificence and suggesting Dante's lines:

> We read of the smile, desired of lips long-thwarted
> Such smile, by such a lover kissed away,
> He that may never more from me be parted
> Trembling all over, kissed my mouth. I say
> The book was Galleot, Galleot the complying
> Ribald who wrote; we read no more that day.

(Inferno (V, 133-138) Transl.: Dorothy L. Sayers, Penguin Books, 1960.)

II *A New Collection*

A publication of a new edition of collected works is always a solemn moment for any writer, a moment of triumph and achievement, signifying the appreciation of the reading public. In 1955 Parandowski published his volume of *Selected Writings* with a preface in which he reviewed his literary activity of the past forty years. The collection pointed to the totality and harmony of his images and to his preoccupation with style which would not tolerate any hastiness, exaggeration or flabbiness of sentiment. Parandowski's style and language were distinguished by restraint and economy; in the choice of his topics the writer always looked for something new and untrodden.

The preface to the volume served as an expression of Parandowski's aesthetic and literary credo, an explanation of his creative activity, comparing it to an arras which was slowly filled with ornament, design and color. The hues have changed from light-hearted frivolity in the beginning to a more sombre color later on in life. The recent cataclysm of the war left an indelible impression on the man. And yet looking back at his characters, Parandowski pointed out that he always was at home with them and, if it were possible, would be happy to invite them for a visit, something that could not always be said about the characters of other writers. The arras was brimful of life in all its manifestations; it glistened like the variegated minerals of Adalbert Stifter, breathed the coolness and viridescence of the southern spring. Its most important component was man, whose footsteps Parandowski has followed from the Stone Age to our century, sometimes with anxiety but always with a firm belief that man's creative ability was stronger than his urge to destroy.

The publication of these *Selected Writings* was greeted with several short and generally friendly reviews of an informative kind.[9] A number of critics reviewed Parandowski's past literary output, comparing him to the men of the Renaissance,[10] and calling him a great classicist and poet.[11] However in 1957, when the writer published a more complete edition in three volumes, he became the object of polemical and vitriolic criticism in *Tworczosc* (creative work), one of the leading literary periodicals.

The controversy began with the publication of a lengthy article entitled *Podroz do Arkadii* (The Trip to Arcadia) by

W. Maciag. More than an ordinary review, it covers practically all of Parandowski's creative output. The reviewer writes convincingly, and as another critic remarked, with a great passion. He begins by praising Parandowski, claiming he is an exceedingly popular writer in Poland; he has admirers and even a following. And yet his name is neglected by any serious criticism. Imperceptibly the reviewer then moves on to severe criticism, stating that on close examination Parandowski's writings prove to be artificial, cerebral and bookish; they smack of academe. "The literature in his writings lost its cognitive value, it became a collection of words, the sole task of which is the beauty of the description."[12] (Similar criticism was repeated almost verbatim much later by Jerzy Putrament in his evaluation of Parandowski's writings.[13]) In spite of occasional coruscation, continues Maciag, his writings are devoid of real life. To him literature is an abstract entity, esoteric, with writers serving the role of an order of priesthood.

Parandowski, according to the reviewer, wrote two biographies, but despite the many years since the publication of the first (on Oscar Wilde), his style has hardly changed in the second, *Petrarch*. Here Maciag makes the cardinal mistake of entering into comparative criticism: the *King of Life* was an excellent work, the cold detached style admirably interpreted the milieu of the late Victorian era as well as the personality of Wilde. In *Petrarch*, however, the same detachment, he says, leads to a certain debilitation and misrepresentation of Petrarch's character. Admittedly *Petrarch* is a work of compilation, but then the writer did not attempt to create an exhaustive biography and produced instead, a brilliant if somewhat lengthy sketch. It is hardly fair to criticize one work only because another is a masterpiece or, because of certain flaws in one piece, to denigrate and reject the writer's entire creative output.

Parandowski's equanimity and his apparent indifference to tragedy and therefore to man, are distressing to Maciag. Continuing his one-sided arguments and Procrustean methods, Maciag makes his final, most damaging, not to say insulting, pronouncement: Parandowski is not a writer but a popularizer of literature.

In the next issue of the same periodical appeared an article by Zdzislaw Najder which came to Parandowski's defense.[14]

Najder agreed with some of the astute observations of his colleague, but contended that his criticism was one-sided. There was nothing wrong with Parandowski's intellectual predilection, as there was nothing wrong with his preoccupation with style and the depiction of the milieu he knew best. Being a humanist was more than mere preoccupation with antiquity; it was a conscious effort to seek peace and harmony in the world. He concluded his article with a statement both stunning and frightening in its veracity: the position of a classicist is difficult, nay, almost impossible in the present-day Poland.

Typical was another article which appeared around the same time.[15] The beginning was laudatory, and its purpose was to dispel certain popular misconceptions about the writer. Parandowski, according to the reviewer, Ryszard Zengel, was an erudite, brilliant humanist, whose works cover an enormous cultural scope; from Homer to James Joyce. Soon, however, the critic made an about-face and claimed that Teofil's conduct and revolt are foreign to modern readers. Neither the positivists nor the existentialists of the present period can resolve a religious conflict, only the Marxists can tackle this problem scientifically and positively.

Disturbed at all the outright criticism and critical equivocation, A. Laszowski joined the fray. The lot of the classicist, he claimed, is a difficult one and he is often misunderstood. A classicist does not participate in world events, he is mainly an observer. The criticism of indifference levelled at Parandowski had been directed before at another poet—no less than Goethe himself. "After all Goethe did not notice the French Revolution" or at any rate did not appreciate its significance. Parandowski, however, is a man of action. Although this is not apparent in his creative writing, it is abundantly manifest in his speeches at various world congresses in which he touches upon the most burning problems of the day.

Laszowski then refutes Maciag *et al* point by point, and reviews once again Parandowski's entire creative output. He reminds the reader that Parandowski's works were often criticized in the past and that the publication of *Heaven in Flames* proved to be an act of civil disobedience and courage when a crowd of pseudo-intellectuals attacked the writer's supposed negation of Catholicism.[16] The article appeared in a Catholic paper, and from this time on Parandowski was more and more drawn to the Catholic press. Almost all of his latest works are published in *Tygodnik Powszechny,* another Catholic newspaper.

"It was during the war that I regained faith," Parandowski claimed at one time. Some critics see in him, notwithstanding the previous Catholic vituperations against him, a Catholic writer from the very beginning of his literary career. There is no doubt that Catholicism had played an important part in his early upbringing, but it was a traditional allegiance. Polish intellectuals, unless they were mystics, usually did not take their Catholicism very seriously and Parandowski was no exception. His friends remember him in his early personal life as an admirer of Dionysus rather than of a mystical god of self-denial. His preoccupation with antiquity exaggerated his rather pagan concept of the world. Culturally he was too astute an intellectual to reject the marvellous period of the pre-Christian ages. And a preoccupation with antiquity which teaches tolerance and understanding for foreign cultures in no way precludes tolerance and acceptance of Christianity. Even Teofil in *Heaven in Flames* is drawn to Poland, deeply rooted in Catholicism. The reconciliation therefore was easy to make in his *Three Signs of the Zodiac.* Parandowski tries to make a synthesis of culture and beliefs; he accepted man in his totality. Christianity to the writer was nothing but a natural sequence of man's development.

During the war, fighting for his own bare existence, shocked by the brutality of men to men, feeling a certain guilt towards his wife, his most trusted and faithful companion, Parandowski must have experienced a deep religious crisis. He never speaks of it, so the very occurrence of the crisis is only a conjecture, but it is a hypothesis supported by others, his friend Wierzynski for example. Out of this maze of personal experiences and possible conversion emerged another book which undoubtedly bears traces of his personal life and which significantly the writer called *Powrot do zycia* (Return to Life). We shall try to establish whether he fulfilled his own expectations or perhaps, because religious experiences are sometimes incompatible with literary expression, he created something which was extraneous to his character as a writer.

CHAPTER 11

Return to Life

THE most persistent theme in contemporary Polish literature is that of war. The occupation, mass executions, destruction of Polish cultural monuments, physical extermination of many Polish intellectuals, the moral degradation of the population all left an indelible mark on the Poles. Again and again Polish writers return to this seemingly permanent obsession.

Parandowski also wrote two books which deal with the time of the occupation. *September Night*, as we have seen, depicts his own personal experiences from the outbreak of the war to the time the family moved out of Warsaw and settled in the country.[1] In his second book on the war, *Powrot do zycia* (Return to Life), which he began to write as early as 1946, Parandowski placed the action in the setting of the family refuge. *Return to Life* is fiction, but Parandowski's experiences in the countryside must have influenced the book.

The plot is very simple: Andrzej Jawien, a famous Polish painter, is taken from a concentration camp to Warsaw to be released because he gained the favor of some Germans with his paintings. The train is attacked by the guerrillas and Jawien escapes, later to be picked up on the road by Professor Bulat who delivers milk to the Germans and whose true identity is unknown to them. He brings the painter to a sanctuary, a small estate which reminds the reader both of the atmosphere of Mickiewicz's *Pan Tadeusz* and of Boccaccio's *Decameron*, for on the estate lives a small colony of people, reminiscent of Boccaccio's characters who ran away from the dreaded plague to wait for the end of the war.

Jawien recovers his health, participates in walks and talks, falls in love with one of the ladies. As he paints her portrait, a stray German enters, destroys the painting and shoots the artist.

137

Gravely wounded, he is taken in by the guerrillas and nursed to health by Irena, his love. They get married. Meanwhile Russian troops arrive and liberate the countryside. The trials and tribulations of the couple are not over, yet they move away from the front line, happy to be alive. To Irena the escape has an added significance for she feels the stirring of a new life in her, justifying the title of the novel.

Jawien and his wife return to a more or less tolerable physical existence. Man however does not live by bread alone and so Parandowski presents and develops another problem: that of the artist in this artificial war-time society. Jawien, the painter, is accepted within the shortest possible time by peasants and sophisticated ladies alike. Watched over and protected by the partisans, he is excluded from their ranks, not for want of trust, but because, as the head of the guerrilla detachment informs him, he is too valuable a man; after all his paintings were being exhibited and discussed in Paris and London.

The leader of the underground movement in the district, Teofil Grodzicki (yes, the same Teofil), appears only twice in the novel although he is discussed several times; Jawien, his university friend, notices a radical metamorphosis in Teofil; he is as pious and blindly religious as any peasant in the country. One of the Polish critics acutely observed that Teofil's conversion should not be surprising; even in *Heaven in Flames* there were indications that his rebelliousness might turn into a reconciliation.[2] But because the reader has been unable to follow Teofil's religious evolution, it is difficult for him to accept this volte-face. He might also have added that the author's deterministic philosophy is difficult to grasp.

Parandowski concludes his book by stating that although the new day was breaking, yet the Germans continued to kill, the smokestacks of crematoriums were still working. The fate of men is predetermined from above, but like ants they do not comprehend, and gropingly try to find their way. It is difficult to judge whether this pronouncement signifies Christian resignation or pagan acceptance of fate. Hence the author does not really convey his own great religious experience and, as in the case of Tolstoy's *Resurrection*, which he used as an ideological vehicle, the reader may well feel that, in spite of occasional brilliant passages in *Return to Life*, the writer fails to be convincing. Parandowski himself sensed it and admitted that no matter how often he felt like returning to his original hero, *Return to Life* dealt with matters different from those in *Heaven in Flames*, was a novel of completely different dimensions and therefore, without any invidious comparisons, should be judged differently.

In the subsequent years the writer edited and published a number of books, compilations and retrospective collections: passages of memoirs, early reviews and a volume of *Juvenilia*. A play, *Medea*, again indicated his interest in experimenting with genres new for him. This was followed by *Kiedy byłem recenzentem* (When I Was a Reviewer) announcing his renewed interest in theater. Parandowski then wrote two more stories.[3] Both could be incorporated into the *Sundial*, but he hopes with good reason (the hero is of pubescent age, somewhat older than the hero of the *Sundial*) to publish them in a collection under the title of the first, *Akacja*. Judging from the first two stories, Parandowski's style in the genre is by no means spent and the reader may expect another masterpiece.

CHAPTER 12

Conclusion

IN the 1960's Parandowski's life is uneventful. He travels a
great deal and, although aloof from politics, his literary
endeavor is officially honored: on July 16, 1959 he was decorated
with the order of *Polonia Restituta;* and in December of 1963
the Banner of Labor was bestowed upon him. Poles abroad also
expressed their appreciation by bestowing upon him the Alfred
Jurzykowski Foundation Millennium Award for 1966, in New
York. The speeches made by friends and critics at these presenta-
tions were not only a worthy tribute to a great writer celebrating
the fiftieth anniversary of his creative activity, but also an in-
dication of his significance in Polish literature.

Parandowski was hailed as a great propagandist of antiquity
and a creator of some of the most magnificent pieces of Polish
prose. The essay, the sketch, the literary travelogue, the excursion
into history, any of these might be called the writer's favorite
genre. Since his collections of essays or sketches very often com-
prise an integrated whole the collection thus becomes an epic
novel, though not in the conventional style of an epic. *Heaven
in Flames* was Parandowski's only novel written in a traditional
style, but still the writer considers this genre the most tenacious,
durable and promising. It was at a time when some modern
critics claimed that because of certain external circumstances,
the novel form was undergoing a disintegration or very radical
transmutation, and its conventional form was being abandoned
for a heterogenous undetermined genre "where elements of
lyricism, essays, pamphlets, monologue and many other kinds increasingly prevail over a central interest in the story, plot, and
definitely profiled characters."[1] When some critics thought that
the "hermetic" and poetic style of plotless fiction was about to
replace the traditional novel, Parandowski unequivocally replied:

Only the novel gives a plastic picture of the customs, technique of life, and social changes, both in synthesis and in analysis, pursuing those countless details that form the mosaic of time. Only the novel bends over the individual in his singular existence, in his inner and outer conflicts and shows the truth about the indestructibility of human substance in the constant desires, passions, regressions, and great achievements. This is the long recognized truth, that in essence man always remains the same in the changing game of millennia, but evidently this truth must be recalled to mind since the suspicion has been expressed that the individual somehow deprives himself of his eternal rights, thus the novel about the individual will soon become impossible. I believe the contrary: never before perhaps has the novel about the individual had more to say and to reveal. . . . The novel is the most elastic literary form, it tends to make and is capable of making all kinds of changes and experiments. And that is why it so attracts writers, not all, of course; some like Paul Valéry will always regard it with disdain and I myself admit (perhaps this is a sign of the times?) that in considering subjects that come to my mind I feel some impatience at the thought of the necessity of thinking out stories for them.[2]

The Mediterranean basin, the cradle of European civilization, has been an inexhaustible source of inspiration for many of Parandowski's works. In this he is a great follower in the historical Polish humanistic tradition. Parandowski is a humanist in his world outlook and a classicist in his writings. As such Parandowski not only celebrates the theme of antiquity, which predominates in his writing, but affirms in sculptured outline a comprehension of the world in its totality through the perception of a calm, seemingly detached, creative and scholarly artist. Yet the writer's ideological make up was by no means static; it changed throughout the fifty years of his creative activity. But what is more important, the country of his birth changed and entered new experiences which came with bewildering rapidity. Still, if for some impatient critics Parandowski did not keep abreast of the times, his classical "rigidity" nevertheless stressed the lasting, universal aspects of our culture and civilization.

As to the problem of estrangement of man from man and the relationship of the writer to any man and every man, Parandowski in his acceptance speech for the honor bestowed upon him for his fiftieth anniversary reiterated his humanistic credo:

I had, of course, my guiding compass, my faith in mankind. I have lived with man through all his transformations, from the days when he held in his hands a rough fragment of stone. I have watched him with great emotion during the dreadful moments when he stood over the precipice, only to transplant himself a moment later to a new higher place and to become triumphant with life and civilization, resplendent with new ideas, sparkling like stars over his head, and raising a new truth which he had unravelled from the mystery of the universe. This is how it was, this is how it is, how it will always be, in this miraculous epic that man creates under the boundless horizon with his life, his destiny and his thoughts.[3]

A retrospective glance over the events of Parandowski's life reminds us that he has been acquainted with the lowest as well as with the highest works of man: the horrors of the German occupation of Poland as well as the glories of Mediterranean civilization. In Poland he has at times been attacked and at times praised. Although the public has never spoken with unanimous voice, he has never entirely lacked defenders and never entirely escaped denigrators. And his own tone has often been equivocal. His most famous book, *Heaven in Flames* depicts Teofil's divine aspirations at the moment of surrendering his religion. His early biography of Oscar Wilde, *King of Life* presents a lost soul surrounded by shreds of glory. For all his devotion to the classics of Greece and Rome, for all his stoic temperament and Attic detachment, did Parandowski fall short of classic stature in his own work? This question only the future may answer. In Parandowski's unyielding dedication to the craft of letters, in his recreation of classical mythology for twentieth-century Poland, in the perspicuous strength to which he has tempered the Polish language—in these are the claims which encourage us to proclaim that a classic Polish writer has appeared in our lifetime and is still among us.

Notes and References

Chapter One

1. Unless otherwise noted, biographical details in this book are from my interviews with Jan Parandowski in 1960 and 1962.
2. Jan Parandowski, *Dziela wybrane*, Warsaw, 1956, 3 volumes. Vol. 3, p. 165.
3. Waclaw Lednicki, "Aleksander Lednicki," *Zeszyty Historyczne*, (1962), pp. 76–77.
4. Zygmunt Nagorski, Sr., "Aleksander Lednicki (1886–1934)," *Zeszyty Historyczne*, (1962), p. 51.
5. A detailed account of the battle is given by Rosa Bailly, *A City Fights for Freedom*, London, 1956.
6. Jan Parandowski, *Juvenilia*, Warsaw, 1960, p. 243.
7. Kazimierz Czachowski, *Obraz wspolczesnej literatury polskiej*, Warsaw-Lwow, 1936, p. 139.
8. See especially the stories of Hermaphroditus (IV) and Anaxarete (XIV).
9. W. Feldman, *Wspolczesna literatura polska*, Lwow, p. 554.

Chapter Two

1. Leslaw M. Bartelski, "An Hour with Jan Parandowski," *Polish Perspectives*, (December, 1959), p. 32.

Chapter Three

1. Jan Parandowski, "Spotkanie z Joycem" (Meeting James Joyce,) *Dziela*, v. 3, pp. 468–477.
2. In 1927 Kazimierz Wierzynski treated a similar theme in a collection of poems, *Laur Olimpijski* (The Olympic Laurel). However, it dealt with the modern Olympic games.
3. *The Olympic Discus*, London, 1939, p. 9.
4. *Ibid*, pp. 9–10.
5. *Dziela*, v. 3, p. 174.
6. *The Olympic Discus*, p. 15.
7. *Ibid*, pp. 45–46.

8. *Ibid*, p. 46.
9. *Ibid*, p. 82.
10. *Ibid*, p. 118.
11. *Ibid*, pp. 118–119.
12. *Ibid*, p. 119.
13. *Ibid*, p. 123.
14. *Ibid*, p. 244.
15. *Ibid*, p. 245.
16. *Ibid*, pp. 249–250.
17. *Ibid*, pp. 139–140.
18. Jan Parandowski, *Podroze literackie*, Wroclaw, 1958, p. 91.
19. Jan Parandowski, "Przygoda z ksiazka," *Kultura*, nr. 1 (30) (1964), p. 3.

Chapter Four

1. Jan Parandowski, *Niebo w plomieniach*, Warsaw, 1952, p. 161.
2. *Niebo w plomieniach*, p. 144. (This, and the other quotations from *Heaven in Flames*, is my own translation).
3. *Ibid*, p. 145.
4. Jan Parandowski, "Roscher," *Polish Perspectives*, Nr. 12 (20), p. 27.
5. *Niebo w plomieniach*, pp. 57–58.
6. Silvester, "Jan Parandowski—Niebo w plomieniach," *Verbum*, III (1936), pp. 537–553.
7. Jan Lorentowicz, "Niebo w plomieniach," *Nowa Ksiazka*, (1936) pp. 465–466.
8. Bronislaw Wojcik, "Gdzie sa pisarze katoliccy?" *Sodalis Marianus*, nr. 12 (1936), p. 8.
9. Jerzy Andrzejewski, "Plomienie bez ognia," *Prosto z Mostu*, R. 2: nr. 38 (1936), p. 5.
10. M. Skudlik, "Bezboznictwo w rekawiczkach," *Przeglad Katolicki*, R. 75, nr. 45 (1937), p. 750.
11. Maria Manteufflowa, "Niebo w plomieniach Jana Parandowskiego," *Prad*, R. 24: z. 1, (1937), pp. 23–26.
12. A. S. Aston, "Bluzniercza powiesc," *Przeglad Katolicki*, n. 8 (1936), p. 134.
13. *Ibid*, no. 11, p. 182.
14. *Ibid*, no. 12, p. 200.
15. *Ibid*, no. 8, p. 135.
16. *Ibid*, no. 12, p. 201.
17. J. N., "O recenzji Astona," *Mlodziez Katolicka*, nr. 4, (1936), p. 25.
18. *Ibid*, p. 25.

19. Zenon Zimorowicz, "O reglamentacji w kulturze umyslowej," *Pro Christo*, R. 14, nr. 3 (1938), p. 25.

20. Bronislaw Wojcik, "Gdzie sa pisarze katoliccy?", *Sodalis Marianus*, nr. 12 (1936), p. 8.

21. *Niebo w plomieniach*, p. 5.

22. Emil Breiter, "Walka z Bogiem o Boga," *Wiadomosci Literackie*, R. 13, n. 28 (1936), p. 4.

23. K. Czachowski, *Najnowsza polska tworczosc literacka*, Lwow, 1938, p. 71.

24. Jan Kulig, "O Janie Parandowskim," *Tygodnik Powszechny*, no. 20 (1963), p. 4.

Chapter Five

1. *Dziela*, v. 2, p. 237.

2. *Ibid*, p. 238.

3. *Ibid*, p. 238.

4. A Polish scholar, in a very interesting and detailed study, sees in this episode a device of juxtaposition so characteristic in Parandowski's writings. We rather think that it is a physical object (the writer uses them often) which brings associations and makes the method of fenestration and projection into the past possible. See Eugenia Wojcikowna, "Glowne tendencje artystyczne w tworczosci Jana Parandowskiego," *Roczniki Humanistyczne*, No. 1 (1961), p. 93.

5. A more indigent account on Aristides is given by Cornelius Nepos.

6. The oath Plutarch alludes to is contained in the *Iliad* I/239: "and this shall be a great oath before you; some day, longing for Achilles will come to the sons of the Achaians, all of them. Then stricken at heart though you be, you will be able to do nothing, when in their number before man-slaughtering Hector they drop and die."

7. Plutarch, *Lives* (New York, The Modern Library), p. 396.

8. Compare also *Moje poczatki literackie* (My Literary Beginnings). *Dziela*, V. 3, p. 162.

9. "Sir Baron call me thou, then is the matter good/ A cavalier am I, like other In my bearing/ Thou has no doubts about my noble blood/ See, here is the coat of arms that I am wearing." (Goethe, *Faust*, 1–6).

10. B. Brecht, *The Life of Galileo*, London, 1963, p. 10.

11. It should be noted that if some readers feel that Parandowski is too Catholic in his collection, certain circles might consider him not Catholic enough. The German edition of *Drei Tierkreiszeichen* (Bibliotheca Christiana, 1962) had the story "The Encyclopedists" deleted from the collection.

Chapter Six

1. This, and some of the other information in this chapter, comes from Parandowski's unpublished diary.
2. Jan Parandowski, *Wrzesniowa noc*, Warsaw, 1962, pp. 14–15.
3. *Ibid*, p. 21.
4. *Ibid*, p. 21.
5. From the unpublished diary.
6. *Ibid*.
7. Interview, Warsaw, July 10, 1962.
8. Interview, Warsaw, July 1, 1962.
9. Interview, Warsaw, July 1, 1962.

Chapter Seven

1. Quoted to me by Zbigniew Folejewski to whom Parandowski said it during an interview.
2. Parandowski retained this reserved attitude towards Sartre, both the man and the writer. In the summer of 1962 Sartre and Simone de Beauvoir stopped in Warsaw on the way from Moscow. Several press conferences (to which I was invited) and receptions were given in honor of the couple. Parandowski, usually an easily accessible and friendly person, neither invited Sartre to the Polish PEN Center nor accepted any invitation to meet him.
3. *Podroze literackie*, p. 216.
4. Maria Kuncewicz, ed. *The Modern Polish Mind*, Boston, Toronto, 1962, p. 3.
5. F. W., "Cenne wznowienie beletrystyczne," *Ksiazka i Kultura*, nr. 7/8 (1947), p. 17.
6. Marian Prominski, "Niebo w plomieniach," *Przekroj*, nr. 100, (1947), p. 20.
7. Jerzy Gembicki, "Niebo w plomieniach," *Zycie Warszawy*, nr. 98 (1947), p. 3.
8. Jadwiga Kulczycka-Saloni, "Wznowione powiesci Parandowskiego," *Kuznica*, nr. 41 (1948), p. 8.
9. Stefan Papee, "Niebo w plomieniach dyskusji," *Rzeczpospolita*, nr. 176 (1947), p. 4.
10. Boguslaw Grodzicki, "Artykul dyskusyjny," *Slowo Powszechne*, nr. 353 (1949), p. 3.
11. Adolf Sowinski, "Perspektywy na Niebo w plomieniach," *Nowiny Literackie*, nr. 10 (1948), p. 2.
12. Mieczyslaw Jaroslawski, "Na marginesie rzeczywistosci," *Tygodnik Wybrzeza*, nr. 36/37 (1949), p. 7.
13. *Ibid*, p. 7.

14. Zofia Starowieyska-Morstinowa, "Poeta wielkiego spokoju," *Tygodnik Powszechny*, nr. 15/16 (1949), pp. 10–11.

15. *Ibid*, p. 7.

Chapter Eight

1. Two stories were published before the war: "Max von Trott, Opowiadanie," *Wiadomosci Literackie*, no. 39 (1938), and "Rodecki," *Wiadomosci Literackie*, no. 34 (1939). Both tales deal with human passions and both heroes end tragically.

2. At one time Parandowski was interested in Chekhov and even translated his longer story "Opowiesc nieznajomego (Metamorfoza Rewolucjonisty)," *Dziennik Ludowy*, no. 174–231 (1924).

3. Eugenia Wojcikowna, "Glowne tendencje artystyczne w tworczosci Jana Parandowskiego," *Roczniki Humanistyczne* (Lublin, 1961), p. 75.

4. *Ibid*, p. 75.

5. *Ibid*, p. 73.

6. "Koniec Roschera, o wielkim, slowniku mitologii greckiej i rzymskiej," *Wiadomosci Literackie*, no. 13 (1938).

7. Jan Parandowski, "Roscher," *Polish Perspectives*, no. 12, (1959), p. 24.

8. Jan Parandowski, "Roscher" *op. cit.*, pp. 26–27.

9. See pp. 66–67.

10. Jan Parandowski, "Roscher," *op. cit.*, p. 28.

11. Interview, Vienna, July 20, 1962.

12. Interview, Warsaw, July, 1962.

13. Joseph Conrad, *The Rover*, (J. M. Dent & Sons), p. 2.

14. Jan Parandowski, "Godzina sródziemnomorska," *Dziela*, v. II, p. 557 (transl. by G.H.).

15. Compare the same attitude taken toward the *Iliad:* "Who would guess what kind of *Iliad* people of Homer's generation have known. The same sounds, the same words, the same verses rendered a different vision in different centuries . . ." Jan Parandowski, *Alchemia slowa*, p. 313.

16. Jan Parandowski, "Introduction to the Life and Work of Adam Mickiewicz," *Adam Mickiewicz*, UNESCO, 1955, pp. 14–15.

17. George Harjan, "Jan Parandowski, Alchemia slowa," *Books Abroad*, 32–3 (1958), pp. 266–267.

Chapter Nine

1. Jan Parandowski—letter to the author, May 18, 1964.

2. Interview, Warsaw, June 10, 1962. Parandowski freely admitted that for a long time he was completely indifferent to music; in fact it disturbed his work. Only recently did he begin to appreciate and enjoy it.

Chapter Ten

1. Aside from the introduction he wrote: "O znaczeniu i godnosci tlumacza" (On the Significance and the Dignity of the Translator) and "Homeryckie boje" (On Translating Homer). It would be more fitting to translate the last one "Controversy around Homer."

2. See: "An Hour with Jan Parandowski," *Polish Perspectives*, (December, 1959), p. 30.

3. Jan Parandowski, "Homeryckie boje" *Dziela*, v. 3, p. 253.

4. "On Translating Homer," *O sztuce tlumaczenia*, p. 553.

5. Interview, New York, July, 1964.

6. "An Hour with Jan Parandowski," *Polish Perspectives*, (December 1959), p. 33. Also Interview, Warsaw, July 11, 1962.

7. Jan Parandowski, "Praca nad Petrarka," *Tworczosc*, nr. 1 (1955).

8. A. V., "Petrarka-patron emigrantow," *Kultura*, (Paris), nr. 1–2, (1957), pp. 196–198.

9. Jerzy Krzyszton, "Daje ci koniec zlotej nici," *Dzis i Jutro*, nr. 8, (1955), pp. 1, 4–5.

Zdzislaw Polsakiewicz, "Wiara w czlowieka," *Nowy Tor*, nr. 30 (1956), p. 2.

Jacek Lukasiewicz, "Rozmowa z Teofilem," *Dzis i Jutro*, nr. 8, (1956), pp. 1, 4–5.

Jerzy Kadziela, "Nie zakonczone dzielo klasyka," *Glos Tygodnia*, nr. 13 (1956), p. 2.

10. Zdzislaw Libera, "Jubileusz Jana Parandowskiego," *Polonistyka*, nr. 4 (1955), pp. 72–74.

11. Jaroslaw Iwaszkiewicz, "Parandowski," *Nowa Kultura*, nr. 23 (1955), pp. 1–2.

12. W. Maciag, "Podroz do Arkadii," *Twórczosc*, 8–58, p. 118.

13. Interview, Warsaw, July 11, 1962.

14. Zdzislaw Najder, "Parandowski czyli dola klasyka," *Twórczosc*, nr. 9 (1958).

15. Ryszard Zengel, "Dzielo imponujace," *Wspolczesnosc*, nr. 21 (1958).

16. A. Laszowski, "Klasyk za zycia," *Kierunki*, 11–1 (1959).

Chapter Eleven

1. Published in 1962 although some of the stories were written before and published as early as 1947.

2. Tomasz Burek, "Odmiany bohatera," *Twórczosc*, (June, 1962) p. 116.

3. Jan Parandowski, "Akacja," *Twósczosc*, 1 (1964). "Figliulo," *Tygodnik Powszechny*, nr. 241 (1964). In 1967 Parandowski pub-

lished under the title *Akacja* a small collection of short stories in which the above mentioned works were included. See: *Akacja*, Warsaw, 1967.

Chapter Twelve

1. E. E. Noth, "The Novel Today, Death or Transmutation," *Books Abroad*, 32–2, p. 117.

2. Jan˙ Parandowski, "The Novel Today," *Books Abroad*, 32–3, p. 241.

3. Jan Parandowski, *Luzne kartki*, Wroclaw, 1965, p. 226.

Selected Bibliography

PRIMARY SOURCES

"Rousseau. Szkic literacko-filozoficzny." *Przeglad,* Lwow 1913.
"Antinous w aksamitnym berecie." [Oscar Wilde] *Gazeta Lwowska*
    1920. No. 279–291. Lwów 1921.
"Rzym czarodziejski." *Biblioteka Teczowa* No. 4. Lwów 1924.
Eros na Olimpie. Lwów 1924.
Mitologia, Wierzenia i podania Greków i Rzymian. Lwów 1924.
Aspazja. Lwów 1925.
Dwie wiosny. Lwów 1927.
Krol zycia. [Oscar Wilde], Lwów 1930.
Wojna trojanska. Opowiedziana dla mlodziezy wedlug "Iliady"
    Homera. Lwów (around 1930).
Dysk olimpijski. Warsaw 1933.
Odwiedziny i spotkania, Warsaw 1934.
Niebo w plomieniach, Warsaw 1936.
Trzy znaki zodiaku. Warsaw 1938.
Godzina sródziemnomorska. Warsaw 1949.
Alchemia slowa. Warsaw 1951.
Zegar sloneczny. Warsaw 1953.
Petrarka. Warsaw 1956.
Pisma wybrane. Warsaw 1955.
Dziela wybrane. Vols. 1–3. Warsaw 1957.
Podróze literackie. Wroclaw 1958.
Mój Rzym. Poznan, 1959.
Wspomnienia i sylwety. Wroclaw 1960.
Juvenilia. Warsaw 1960.
Powrót do zycia, Poznan, 1961.
Wrzesniowa noc. Warsaw 1962.
Medea. Warsaw 1962.
Kiedy bylem recenzentem. Warsaw 1963.
Luzne kartki. Wroclaw 1965.
Akacja. Warsaw 1967.

SECONDARY SOURCES

Reviews and Articles

ANDRZEJEWSKI, J. "Plomienie bez ognia." *Prosto z mostu*, 1936, nr. 38.
BREITER, E. "Walka z Bogiem o Boga." *Wiadomosci Literackie*, 1936, nr. 38.
HARJAN, G. "J. Parandowski: Dziela wybrane." *Books Abroad* 32/4, 1958.
———. "Parandowski: a Contemporary Polish Humanist." *Books Abroad* 34/3, 1960.
———. Introduction to the *Olympic Discus*, New York, 1964.
———. "Odwiedziny i spotkania z Janem Parandowskim," *Glos Polski* nr. 48, Toronto, 2.12.1965.
JAROSLAWSKI, M. "Na marginesie rzeczywistosci. O filozofii J. Parandowskiego." *Tygodnik Wybrzeza* 1948 nr. 36–37. *Rocznnik tow. Nauk. Warsz.* R. 41: 1948 pp. 69–72.
IWASZKIEWICZ, J. "Parandowski." *Nowa Kultura* 1955, nr. 23.
KULIG, JAN. "Miedzy dwoma swiatami." *Tygodnik Powszechny* 20–1965.
LASZOWSKI, A. "Klasyk za zycia." *Kierunki* 11.1.1959.
MACIAG, W. "Podróz do Arkadii." *Twórczosc* 8–1958.
NAJDER, Z. "Parandowski czyli dola klasyka." *Twórczosc* 9–1958.
NAPIERSKI, S. "Parandowski humanist." *Bunt Mlodych* 1937 nr. 2.
ROMAINS, J. "Un grand écrivain polonais à Paris." *Nouvelles Littéraires* 1 V 1937.
STAROWIEYSKA-MORSTINOWA, Z. "Poeta wielkiego spokoju." *Tygodnik Powszechny* 1949 nr. 15/16, "Wedrówka przez stulecia." *Radio i Swiat* 1954 nr. 46.
———. "Slowo laskawe i kojace." *Kalejdoskop literacki*. Warsaw 1955, pp. 170–190.
SUBOTIN, STOJAN. Knjizevno stvaralstvo Jana Parandovskog. *Delo* Belgrade. June 1962.
WOJCIKOWNA, E. Glówne tendencje, artystyczne w twórczosci Jana Parandowskiego. *Roczniki Humanistyczne* Lublin 1961.
ZENGEL, RYSZARD. Dzielo imponujace. *Wspólczesnosc* nr. 21, 1958. (Review of Parandowski's Selected Works).

Works Translated into English

The Olympic Discus, London, 1939.
The Olympic Discus, New York, 1964.
"Introduction to the Life and Work of Adam Mickiewicz." *Adam Mickiewicz*, UNESCO, 1955.
"The Novel Today," *Books Abroad*, 32–3. Norman, Oklahoma.

"The Third Spring," *Poland*, Warsaw, 51, Nov. 1958, 12–16, 25–26.

"Roscher," *Polish Perspectives*, Dec. 1959. 24–28.

"A Thousand Years of Latin," *Poland*, Warsaw, 67, Mar., 1960, 16.

"An Ordinary Day," *Introduction to Modern Polish Literature*, eds. Adam Gillon & Ludwik Krzyzanowski, Twayne Publ., New York, 1964.

Index